THE MAGNOLIA CODE

THE MAGNOLIA CODE

JOAN BROOKS BAKER

With best wishes to Glap — thanks for your enthusiasm!

Joan Brooks Baker

FRESCO BOOKS

Mama may have, Papa may have
But God bless the child that's got his own

Billie Holiday — *God Bless the Child*

Finally and always for Margeaux

MMXXX

Publisher
SF Design / Fresco Books
Albuquerque, New Mexico
frescobooks.com

Edited byHollis Walker

Printed and bound in Italy
ISBN: 978-1-934491-68-3
Library of Congress Cataloging in Publication: 2019917375

Cover: A photographic collage of *A View of New York
Among the New Mexico Trees*

Some names and locations have been changed to
protect the privacy of those concerned.

CONTENTS

1

Isaiah

I never saw Isaiah mad, even when Mother asked him to do five things all at the same time. "EYE-ZEER," she would call out. This mispronunciation of his name drove my sisters and me crazy.

"His name is Isaiah—Eye-ZAY-uh," we enunciated with adolescent irritation. But she ignored us. In fact, they both ignored us. Mother and Isaiah—a black man who had grown up in Jacksonville, Florida—had a bond so strong that Mother's soft North Carolina accent took on some of Isaiah's cadence when they talked together.

It was early fall, 1959. I was fifteen years old, preparing to leave home in New York for my first year at boarding school in Massachusetts. Anxious for the change, angry that my two older sisters had left me alone with my bickering parents—Alicia had already gone off to her boarding school and Barrett had recently married—I was ready for new surroundings. The day before, on my way to my room to finish the school's dreaded summer reading, I stopped unseen at the end of the kitchen hallway to listen to the easy chatter of Mother and Isaiah.

The kitchen was toward the back of the apartment. The sounds of the car horns on Park Avenue blowing their impatience and the trains rumbling on the rails under the median created a constant hum, but Mother and Isaiah didn't let the noise bother them. They were immersed in their own putterings. Preparing ten prune cakes for the Fifth Avenue Presbyterian Church Fair that coming weekend captured their full attention. Mother and the other volunteer women were proud of the money they earned for the "meal outreach."

Isaiah with my nephew

Mother and Isaiah always shared the labor of the Prune Cake Project. Her recipe—on a card smudged with old food spills—sat propped up against the salt-and-pepper shakers. She never looked at the recipe. She just put in what seemed to be the right amounts: two cups of Presto Self-Rising Cake Flour, a "world" of sugar, some cinnamon, nutmeg, and ground cloves, and, of course, a jar of Gerber's pureed prune baby food. Crisco also played an important role, as it did in most any Southern cooking. Isaiah tried to make sure the spices weren't just flung in.

"Miss Alice, that's just not balanced right," he would say. "Let's put in some more cinnamon." He paid special attention to the timing and temperature of the oven, knowing that Mother had a habit of leaving the kitchen for "five minutes" that turned into twenty.

After the cakes were out of the oven, Mother cooled them on wire racks, finally transferring them onto paper plates, ready for Saturday, two days hence. At the fair, she stood behind the booth, selling at a good pace, always making sure to share the baking credits with Isaiah. She had to. Isaiah's cooking had a reputation.

Nothing seemed to bother Isaiah, not my mother's mispronunciation of his name or her haphazard lifestyle. His patient face hid a smile waiting to be realized, and he remained calm even in the middle of their baking, when Mother would suddenly put down the wooden spoon, remembering an urgent task.

"Eye-zeer, I need your help. I almost forgot, I must go across town to the thrift store to return this big box of china. Remember? I bought it yesterday, but it's all wrong. That nice man, Sam, he said I could bring it back, but to do so right away. Now don't tell Mrs. Thompson."

Isaiah knew that Mother's best friend, Mrs. Thompson, could embarrass her, especially when Mother bought things she didn't really want or care about.

"No'm," Isaiah told Mother, "just made a mistake, that's all. No one needs to know everything."

"Can you go get the car? If you would do just this one thing for me, that's all I ask."

"I will, Miss Alice. Let me put these dishes away, then I'll get my driving jacket." Isaiah spoke with amused resignation as he quietly figured out how he was going to put the afternoon in order.

"My errand won't take long. Then I will have to stop by the grocery for just a minute. I forgot the ice cream for tonight."

Isaiah shook his head and breathed out a soft hum.

"That's fine, I do thank you, I really do," Mother said. "Now, if you would just get the car and not take too long, I am ready. I'll get myself together, take off this apron—you laugh when I forget to do that," she said, giving Isaiah a quick smile. "Then I'll go choose a hat."

"Oh, Lord, there's the telephone," Mother called out to the apartment.

Isaiah joined our family in 1954 when I was ten, Alicia twelve, Barrett eighteen. He had worked for Father's parents in Jacksonville. When they died, Father asked Isaiah to come to New York.

"Going north to the big city will be an adventure," Isaiah told my cousins when they asked how he could possibly leave his good life with them down South for "those Yankees."

Isaiah had presence. He expertly walked the fine line between a "best-to-know-your-place" servant and a self-possessed man. I believe he liked us, but I believe even more that he "saw" us, understood each one of us, his white-people family. He knew little things about us and he cared. To Alicia and me one morning, he said with a big smile, "I brought y'all some more goldfish for your fish tank." Sometimes he asked which teachers we liked the best and why, or what the tough subjects were at school.

I look back and realize that we didn't, for the most part, "see" Isaiah—it didn't occur to us, really—other than to recognize him in his role as the wonderful man who came to our apartment in the morning, took care of us, and at night went to his home, somewhere uptown. His life was worlds away from my family's.

"That's just how it is," Mother would say.

There wasn't room in our apartment for Isaiah, even if he had wanted to live with us, which he didn't. He wanted to live in Harlem, and he found himself a good place—so my parents said—on 121st Street on the West Side. Definitely he would choose to live on the West Side, or in Central Harlem; the East Side was Spanish Harlem. Isaiah knew where he belonged.

He was a handsome man, a bit of a dandy, a "dresser." At age eleven or so, I once told him, "You look like a sun-tanned movie star." He laughed. I remember his long, graceful fingers, one bearing what looked like a signet ring. When leaving our apartment to go up to his place, he sported the latest-in-fashion straw hat, and his brown-and-white spectator shoes were always polished to the hilt. Long and lanky, he walked with pride, wearing a smart pair of yellow-tinted sunglasses just like Father's.

I didn't tell Isaiah I loved him, but I did. His easy way made me want to be with him, sit with him in the kitchen and ask endless questions. My parents said I shouldn't be so personal.

"Be proper, Joanie. Let him have his life. He doesn't want you to ask and there's nothing we need to know," Mother admonished.

I tried not to be personal, but I was curious and longed to picture his life.

"What's your apartment like? What's the view? Do you have friends? Does anyone come for Sunday supper on your day off?" I loved to sit with him after school——me in my fourth-grade uniform, he in his white jacket, his "inside-the-apartment uniform," as he called it. He described the dances he went to, the street games, the clothes people wore. I'd seen photographs of the black church women and I wanted to know details about the shapes and colors that topped the heads of both women and men in his church, the Abyssinian Baptist Church on 136th Street. He described the Harlem streets, vendors on the sidewalk selling magic potions "that will make men spin for the scent of you," hawkers selling the lottery ticket that would change your life's fortune, booths of clothes, shoes, and in the summer, fruits and vegetables driven in early from the Bronx. He told me about "stoop life," how in good weather, neighbors sat on the steps going up to the brownstone buildings' entrances. "Community," he called it.

But Harlem wasn't safe, Mother would tell me, without explanation. I didn't understand because Isaiah's Harlem had fun and wonder in it. Later I realized he never talked of the race riots, the Jim Crow laws, or the small but significant victories of the civil rights movement. I didn't know how central Harlem was to the racial changes going on in the country, or whether Isaiah had his own personal troubles.

"Why isn't Harlem safe?" I asked Mother.

"Because I said so, that's why. Life is complicated," she snapped. "Stop asking why all the time," she added in an angry tone that made me back away.

Isaiah, in his own manner, also showed me proper behavior. One summer, having just turned twelve, I climbed into the front seat of Father's Cadillac convertible as I usually did.

"Now, Miss Joanie, I believe it's time for you to sit in the back," Isaiah said.

"Why? I don't want to. I want to sit up here with you."

He responded with almost the same words as Mother's.

"That's just the way it is." But he added gently, "You're older now. Go on back there." Isaiah pulled the red leather seat forward for me to enter the cavernous back.

"Darn, now I can't see you," I complained. "I can't talk to you from here." Isaiah shook himself with a laugh.

Mother had a habit of falling into bad moods. When Isaiah saw her "nervousness," as he called her moods, coming on, he would gently suggest we children stay quiet, and then he would hum a little louder. Humming seemed to secure his privacy and at the same time assured those around him that everything was all right.

One day I asked him what he was humming.

"A hymn we sing in my church. I'm learning the words."

"Oh, sing it to me, Isaiah."

He stroked his forehead the way he always did when he was thinking, and turned his back to me. Chuckling a bit, he slowly sang:

> *Shall we gather at the river,*
> *Where bright angel feet have trod;*
> *With its crystal tide forever*
> *Flowing by the throne of God?*

He stopped. "Oh, I do like that hymn. Reminds me of a river in Jacksonville. Makes me think of my mother. She was such a churchgoer, nearly every day. She liked to hum that tune when she did her gardening."

He picked up a silver plate for polishing and continued humming as he shined it.

"I think Mama liked that hymn because she liked the St. Johns River near her home down there in Jacksonville. She'd take a pillow, sit amongst the palmetto bushes by the banks, and sometimes even take off her shoes and stockings, put her feet in the cool stream. 'That's when I feel good,' she told me, ' 'specially good if the magnolias are in their full bloom.' "

He paused a long time and turned back to his polishing. He said he missed his mother, that he missed all those people he grew up with on Orchard Street.

I waited, hoping he would tell me more.

Hesitating, he looked at the kitchen clock.

"She was the kindest of all. But always running, in a hurry, never did sit down much." He chuckled. He glanced down the kitchen hallway to see, I guessed, if Mother was nearby.

"You know," Isaiah said as he started in on the asparagus washing, "This might seem funny, but your mother sometimes reminds me of my mama, always running, same way in the kitchen, leaving things to be burnt up good, just like the other day with those prune cakes."

He suddenly turned to me, asparagus in his hand, his brow worried with a wrinkle. He said with urgency, "Now, don't you tell your mother I said that. No, don't tell her that."

"Okay," I answered, knowing I wasn't supposed to ask why.

"You'll understand one day," he said, once again echoing Mother. Why couldn't I understand today, I wondered. Why is everything always in the future?

He turned to chopping the vegetables on the small wooden cutting board.

I sat for a while, unsure that he would want to hear my comment, or even believe me.

"You know that hymn, the one you just sang, 'Shall We Gather?' Well, you'll think I'm making this up, but I'm not. Last week Mother and I were crossing in the middle of the street and she said, 'Joanie, don't you jaywalk like I do. It's not right, but I can't help it.' Then she laughed and said, 'But if I do get hit by a Madison Avenue bus, remember to sing that hymn, 'Shall We Gather at the River.' I just heard it again on the radio, reminded me of my old Sunday school days."

Isaiah put down the knife, and looked straight at me, puzzled. Slowly, he said, "Well, I'll be. Now that is something." He wiped his hands on his apron and went back to chopping, all the while humming the hymn.

I knew that Mother and Isaiah came from different worlds, of course, but I saw similarities in their Southernness. Besides her accent sometimes slipping into Isaiah's rhythmic way of speaking, I heard Mother's admiration for the blacks' religious life, even though she never would have visited their church.

"They just have a spirit in them, especially their songs, in their ease. I guess they had to have that," she said with a sigh.

But that appreciation was as much as she could give the black person. She believed in racial separation, thought it was for the best. Later, I came to understand that when Southerners talk about black people being "family," they mean a closeness that has nothing to do with equality. It's a presumptive fantasy. I've never heard black people call the white people for whom they worked "family."

One springtime Sunday in 1961, my sister Barrett and I walked down Madison Avenue after church. We were about the same height, but her heels and recently created high helmet streaked hairdo gave her at least two inches over me.

We looked at store windows full of current fancy outfits, and another with TVs for sale, ten showing the crowd at the previous day's Freedom Ride in Alabama, a bus on fire, chaos, police swinging billy clubs.

Barrett pulled me away from the window, "Come on, let's go, I'm late."

"But can't you wait a minute? Look, this is horrible. You always act like stuff doesn't really matter."

"I don't know what to think. Oh, Joanie, I'm a lot older than you; I have other things on my mind. And I know there's nothing I can do about these problems. And neither can you. Maybe black people should stay with their own, just like people say." I could see Barrett's face tightening when she asked, "Are you a 'Cadillac liberal?' Is that what you want to be, some high and mighty do-gooder who doesn't see reality? I heard you talking to Jane the other day. You better be careful."

My friend Jane's father, a lawyer, was involved with civil rights. He wanted his daughter to know about the cultural changes he hoped were coming.

"Tell your friends, they should know," he told Jane. I liked her father. He treated us like grown-ups.

"Well, maybe I am a ... whatever you called it. I don't know." I didn't want to look at her. "And who are you anyway, just because you're married and live in some fancy uptown apartment."

"Come on, I'm going on down the street," she said, dismissing me.

I followed and wondered about the meaning of "Cadillac liberal." Seeds of doubt undermined my concept of injustice. My rebellious side found an easy counter to the ways I was told to behave, but I wasn't sure of alternative paths, only that I yearned to escape any stifling code of conduct.

Once, on my return from visiting my aunt in the South, Mother cheerfully exclaimed, "And how lucky that you were there in magnolia time! Oh, that divine smell."

But for me the fragrance of magnolias was claustrophobic.

One afternoon after Mother had admonished me yet again for wrongdoing—this time for wearing blue jeans to the grocery store—I mimicked her words to Alicia.

"'It's just not right. It's common,'" one of Mother's favorite words. "I hate Mother's correct ways," I said to Alicia. "Good manners—they're not everything. I want to say and do what I feel, whatever that is."

Alicia mocked me and started singing that song, *I Gotta Be Me*.

"You know, Alicia, it's like the scent of magnolias, that sticky heaviness. I can't breathe."

From then on Alicia and I referred to Mother's unwritten rule book as the "Magnolia Code." From an early age we had been quietly informed that if you follow the rules of the code, you would be given the warmth of a Southern embrace. But if you deviate and turn your back on propriety, you could very well be relegated to the Southern branch of hell.

My conversations with Isaiah became deeper as I grew older. He said he still enjoyed his life in Harlem, but things had changed—more crime, more drugs and danger on the street. That's all he would say. I asked him about his church. Did he still go to the Abyssinian Baptist? Did he still love the singing?

"Oh yes," he said. "That's my community, and I work with the fellowship as much as I can."

I wanted to go up to Harlem to the blues and jazz clubs. I played blues on the piano, and Small's Paradise was the place, a world I wanted to enter, just to see what was happening.

"Is there any way I can go up to a club with some friends? I'm almost eighteen."

"No, no, it's not for you," he said emphatically. He turned away. "You'd be looked at wrong. Anyway, it's not a good time right now in Harlem. You stay with your own."

He didn't often talk to me that way. Usually he was gentler. I felt a blush coming on. I didn't want to seem stupid and look like a little white girl not knowing my place, so I quickly added, "I know what's going on up there. I just wanted to know if I could go to Small's Paradise."

"Now, Miss Joanie, you go on and find places that are right for you and your age."

I left the kitchen. Mother was in the hallway.

"Come into the den, Joanie," she said, steaming with fury. "What's the matter with you? You know you can't go up to Harlem! And that you would ask Isaiah, I'm shocked, furious." She stared at me. I felt small. "There are rules. You better figure out how to live within them." Walking out of the room, Mother looked back at me balefully. "Why do you have to be so different?"

I didn't answer.

Different. What did that mean? I was curious, that's all, just a curious child. I did want to fit in, but in my own way.

Isaiah knew how to fit in. What I was soon to know of his double life would make me admire—even more—his seeming ability to find balance, to negotiate his path. He became a role model and I wanted the kind of self-possession and self-respect he had.

At about the same time, and with my recently unleashed eighteen-year-old wisdom, I had a run-in with Father. We were driving downtown in the blue Cadillac convertible, top down, Isaiah in his black driving jacket and cap and Father in his proper Wall Street suit and dashing Panama hat. I was in the back seat. Sleepy from having stayed out too late and from the luxurious smell of car leather, I half-listened to their chatter and laughter. They had forgotten about me.

Father thought he could say anything to Isaiah because he had pronounced him his best friend. That day in the car he started telling him jokes.

"How many colored men does it take to screw in a light bulb?"

Isaiah gave a small uncomfortable laugh and answered, "Hmmm, Mr. John, how's that?"

"It takes three: one to hold the ladder, one to screw in the light bulb, and the other to sing *Jacob's Ladder*."

"Yes, Mr. John, that's a funny one."

I kept quiet.

"You know, Isaiah, I was thinking about my parents this morning. They were good people," Father mused.

"Yes, sir, they surely was. Kind, always kind to me. Kind to my Aunt Mammy, too."

"Wonderful Mammy. I will never forget that day when my brothers and sisters celebrated her hundredth birthday. Brother Itch asked, 'Mammy, what's my name?' She looked at him like he was crazy and answered, 'Lord, son, if you don't know your name, why should I?' " Father gave out a huge laugh.

I laughed, too. They turned, surprised to find me there.

"She called us her 'chilluns.' I wonder what she'd think of things today," said Father. "All these marches, so much crime up there in Harlem. Not sure she'd be proud of her people today. Is it just bad colored people acting that way, Isaiah?"

I blurted out loudly from the back. "And I hear from Jane's father that the white landlords do nothing about their rotting tenements."

"Joanie, you don't know what you're talking about and neither does Jane's father, whoever he is. You just hush up back there," Father ordered.

Isaiah fiddled with the steering wheel. He adjusted the air conditioning—even though the top was down—and finally said to Father, "Well, I will say that things aren't so good anymore," he said. "Too much danger going on."

"Your people, they are good people, that's for sure, but they ought to take care of their own. Like you do. Is it jobs they want? I could help. Lots of work on Wall Street for porters, waiters in company dining rooms, things like that. Would that help?"

"Yes, sir, Mr. John, that's a fine idea."

Isaiah drove on, the conversation over.

I returned home from college on vacation. Isaiah stood in his white jacket at his usual spot by the kitchen sink, and I sat at the table, dressed in what I hoped was a sophisticated outfit. I now had a tall, athletic body, my thick blonde hair swept into a silver clip at the nape of my neck. Curiosity and feistiness defined parts of me, but my mask of confidence belied an inner lack of worthiness.

Mammy

Familiar cornbread scents wafted from the stove.

"Isaiah, I've never really asked you why you decided to come north. I mean I know my grandparents had died, but why did you leave Jacksonville, all those friends, everything familiar?"

"Oh, you know," he said as he looked into the oven and rearranged the pans. "I just have a restless part of me. I like seeing what's out there. Guess I'm born that way."

"I'm restless, too. Did you know I'm supposed to make my debut this year? It seems stupid, don't you think?"

"Why? Parties sure are fun, I'm positive of that."

"Yes, fun, and now that I'm eighteen I can go to Small's and all those jazz bars and nightclubs. That's part of it. But it sounds awful to be 'presented' like I'm some sort of piece of cake, though my friends are doing it—going to parties, 'bowing' at balls. Bowing—that sounds terrible, too."

"Well, some of that sounds like fun."

I put aside my rebellious urge to mock the debutante in favor of fun and the idea of freedom in New York. And Isaiah helped me dare to act with self-confidence. My best friend Abby was having her big party at the River Club, but my escort had called that morning to say he was sick. Isaiah was in the apartment; my parents were away. I moaned to Isaiah how sad I was to miss Abby's party.

"You go on anyway," Isaiah urged.

"I can't go alone."

"Yes, I believe you can. I'll drive you to the River Club, and I'll promise, if you're not having fun, you can call me to come pick you up." He began humming.

"Isaiah, you would do that?"

He stopped humming long enough to say, "Yes, you want to go. I know."

Sometimes Isaiah had a rough cough. Alicia told me that he'd been sick with tuberculosis before he came north. I asked him if it was true.

"Yes," he answered with a soft hum. "Yes'm, that's right, I was real sick. Your father sent me to the tuberculosis sanatorium over there in west Florida. I stayed three months and they fixed me up pretty good, caught it early. Your father, he was kind to help me like that."

I stayed seated at the table, wondering why I hadn't known about Isaiah's illness or Father's involvement.

"May I ask you, Isaiah, what do you think of civil rights now? I see on TV what's happening—dogs grabbing people, water from the fire hoses knocking over protestors. Do you have hope, Isaiah? Are you proud of your people?"

"Yes, I am proud," Isaiah said, walking over to the cabinets. "Lots happening. Don't know where it's going. Now let me get this cornbread out of the oven; don't want to burn it all up good."

"Isaiah, do you work for 'the rights?' " I asked, using the phrase I had heard him say.

He didn't answer. In my head, I heard Mother chiding me, "Joanie, don't ask Isaiah personal questions."

Giving me a quick glance as he put away the pots, Isaiah said, "When that good man, President Kennedy, got shot a little time ago, that was a terrible, terrible thing for all of us. Now we don't know the future. We pray a lot at my church. We have hope.

"Oh, look at the time. Yes'm, got to go pick up your mother."

"I wish you'd tell me more, Isaiah. Do you have to go right now?"

"One day, I'll tell you some more—one day."

Even as we all grew older, Isaiah's curiosity about our lives remained. He still asked Alicia and me questions.

In the late sixties, I worked for a public interest group—not as a bleeding heart, as my sister Barrett might have called me—but with the intention of learning about other worlds, especially because this particular nonprofit was located in the heart of profit-making Wall Street.

Several times a month I went uptown to visit my parents and stay for dinner. I always went to the kitchen to find Isaiah. His temples had grayed, he had a slight stoop, and now when his glasses slipped down his nose, he let them stay there. His hands rested in his lap, those hands that used to move so fast—dusting, cooking, arranging, grabbing for his keys and his black jacket. He wasn't old, but he seemed worn out. He still hummed, but his humming was quieter and less enthusiastic.

One evening at the apartment, his look startled me. He was thin, wan, unsteady on his feet—and coughing.

"Isaiah, you don't look good."

"Well, no, Miss Joanie, I'm going to tell you that surely I do not feel too good at this moment. I don't know what's got into me, but I best sit down." He sat heavily and leaned his forehead on his hand.

"You better go home," I said.

"Yes, I think so. I'll just finish up with the fixins' here so when your parents get home all will be ready. Lordy, I feel so slowed-down."

I was worried. I should take him home in a cab. But I knew that in his book of "correct behavior," that wouldn't be right. I could hear my parents angrily telling me to stop meddling, "because he can take care of himself." But he looked so weak. We took a taxi up to 121st Street.

The Park Avenue median between the south and north sides of 96th Street marks an enormous crossing into another culture. The trains come up from underground onto the avenue, turning the quiet hum into a clanging. There Spanish Harlem begins: bodegas with olive-skinned people, the end of formal apartment houses, and the start of haphazard buildings. The taxi turned left, into black Harlem.

When the taxi stopped, Isaiah said with as much strength as he could muster, "Thank you, I can get myself up to my apartment." But he could hardly get out of the taxi. I went around to help.

"We'll go upstairs together," I said with unease, looking around me, wondering what people might think of our odd twosome. I could sense him looking also. The six o'clock rush hour from the nearby 125th Street subway exit was underway. Vendors were hawking colorful clothes and pronouncing the ripped-off handbags as "the real stuff." Out of the corner of my eye, I saw three men sitting on rickety chairs banging down their playing cards on a little table. "Ha, there's the card, gin."

Isaiah pulled on my outstretched arm to get his body out of the taxi.

"No, that doesn't look right. You go on home."

"You can't," I protested. "I'll just get you up to your apartment."

The taxi driver asked if he should wait.

"Yes, I'll just be a short time."

We took the elevator. He got out the key and gave it to me to open the door while his other hand steadied him against the wall.

"I'll wait inside for a few minutes, to see how you're doing," I said. "You go lie down."

I heard him sit on his bed with a sigh.

Standing stiffly in his sitting room, I felt caught between the correctness of not trespassing on his privacy and not being able to resist seeing another side of Isaiah. To cross the boundary into his private life in this tidy room was a choice. I wondered for a moment—would Isaiah really mind?

Circumstances, not direct intention, had put me in his apartment, I told myself as my eyes roamed the room. I put my hands on the back of a green over-stuffed chair positioned in front of the TV; fresh cigars and matches were placed neatly on a table next to the chair. The room smelled sweetly of old cigars, and the ceramic ashtray, with a big bird sitting in its center, held a half-smoked stogie, as Isaiah called them. Leaning against the table lamp was a picture of Isaiah, his wife Olivia, and two friends—all dancing—framed by a cardboard nightclub mat with the name "The Big Bird Club" embossed on the bottom. I stood in his room with the ghost of his good times.

Hurrying, afraid Isaiah would catch me looking into his world, I opened the window so the street noises, quickly rising up to the third floor, would cover my steps. A folding card table with four chairs pushed underneath was near the window. A deck of cards waiting to be dealt sat on the table's edge. Positioned on top of an open magazine, with pages torn out, lay a black-and-white photograph of Isaiah's church. On the bottom of the picture was inscribed, "To our friend, Isaiah Stallings, with thanks from our community for your conviction and leadership in the fight against the Harlem landlords. It is you who has made a difference." I stopped and stared at the photograph and felt a dizzying confusion. Isaiah an activist? Deeply involved with the civil rights movement? This side of Isaiah's life seemed so far away from my world. I couldn't put the pieces together.

"Are you still out there, Miss Joanie? I kind of thought you'd be gone," his voice cracked with anxiety.

"Just going now, Isaiah."

I leaned out the window to see if the cab was still waiting. In my hurry, I knocked the magazines and the photograph to the floor. As I knelt to pick up the papers, I felt a longing for something I knew was slipping away. I began to sense the harsh truth, that this connection with Isaiah had been only half real: it had always been focused on me, the little girl in the Park Avenue apartment. I felt lonely. I slowly put everything back as I'd found it. I wanted to leave, go back downtown to the comfort of my upbringing.

"Should I phone a friend of yours to come over?" I quickly called into his room.

He mumbled something about just wanting to sleep. He softly added, "Be careful now. And we'd best keep this quiet, okay, Miss Joanie?"

"Yes, okay, Isaiah," I answered. As I closed the door, I wondered which part he meant to keep quiet.

I ran down the stairs and took the cab to my apartment instead of to my parents', as I had originally planned. I didn't want to talk to them. I didn't want to hear them tell me that what I had done was wrong. And I didn't want to have to concentrate on hiding my new knowledge of Isaiah as an activist.

Isaiah recovered, but he was never quite the same. Soon after the evening in Harlem, I visited my parents and immediately went to the kitchen. Father had put on his new Duke Ellington record and, as usual, it was too loud. I wondered if Isaiah was going to mention my trip to his apartment. Did he wonder if I had told my parents? I sat at the kitchen table and looked down at my hands. I wanted to say something meaningful.

Isaiah looked at me kindly.

"You know, it's time that I return to Jacksonville. I don't feel so very well. So it's not too far off that I'll need to be going on home."

I sat up straight and said too quickly, "Oh, why, Isaiah? You'll be all right. Just wait a little." But a secret place in me had already known. "Yes, I thought soon you'd be telling me that." Tears started behind my eyes. I pushed back my chair and threw my arms around him. "Isaiah, I'll miss you so."

I had never hugged Isaiah before. He stood still and let me hold on for just a moment.

Cactus Pete

2

Cactus Pete

"My name is Cactus Pete," I said, holding back a rising sob.

"And do you know your last name?" asked the woman next to the microphone.

"Yes, well, the doorman calls my mother Mrs. Baker."

"Is there a Mrs. Baker in the store?" the woman asked over the loudspeaker at Best & Co. "If so, please come to the Customer Service desk on the first floor. Your little girl, uh"— she turned to me. "Did you say your name is Cactus Pete?" she asked.

"Yes."

"Of course, dear." She clicked the mic on again. "Mrs. Baker, I repeat, Mrs. Baker, please come to Customer Service. Cactus Pete is here looking for you."

I sat next to the woman, her small working space piled with boxes and a big trashcan overflowing with pieces of paper. My stomach ache had started when I realized I was alone, but I didn't want to announce that I didn't feel well because the woman might look at me with a sad face that would make me cry. While I ran my eyes up and down the aisles, I explained how I had become lost.

"Why did she do that—my mother," I sputtered. "Why did she have to walk so fast —down the street, through the store—so fast. If I stopped for one second, just one second— and this time it was to look at the dancing ballerina in her pink dress—Mother disappeared."

"Did she tell you to hurry?" asked the woman, flipping her cigarette lighter open and shut.

"Yes, she told me to hurry. I know. But I had to stop."

"How old are you, Cactus Pete?"

"I'm six years old, nearly seven. I'll be seven in April."

"I like your very fetching coat, and isn't that something—you have a matching hat."

"I like hats."

"And those leather leggings," she said, pulling out a long, thin cigarette from a Pall Mall pack. "They must keep you warm on a day like this."

"Yes, they're called chaps. Cowboys wear them."

"Yes, yes," she answered, drawing in the smoke and looking around the store. "I'm sure your mother's just as upset as you are. Don't worry, she'll be here any minute."

"I don't know, she might forget. She almost forgot me last week."

"No, don't be silly, of course she won't forget."

We sat in silence for a long minute.

"Look, someone's coming now."

I saw Mother hurrying through the aisles, unbuttoning her big black-and-brown winter coat. She saw me and put her hand to her heart.

"I thought I'd lost you. Yes, I'm Mrs. Baker," she said, turning to the woman while catching her breath. I quickly got out of the chair to run toward her. Then the tears started.

"Cactus Pete is brave. She's been waiting quietly," said the woman. "We were both a bit worried; the store is so crowded during the holidays."

"Thank you for taking care of her. We'll go more slowly now, Joanie."

Mother didn't call me Cactus Pete; that was my father's name for me. She didn't see me as a cowgirl. Though she walked slower, she started talking fast.

"We'll pass through the perfume section and you can spray the bottles. We'll try on some hats, those funny big hats, you love hats. Then we'll go wherever you want for lunch."

It was 1950, and in those days Mother was distracted—with me, anyway. She always seemed to be somewhere else. On one particularly bad day, my sister Alicia and I thought maybe Mother had other children somewhere—a secret life. I would come to understand that she didn't want another life; she just didn't feel comfortable in the one she had. Always correct and proper, it didn't occur to her she might have other options. How could she know? How could any woman know, in the rigid culture of 1950s America, that there was something more? Anyway, when she married Father at the age of twenty, and for quite a long time after, her choice must have seemed a good one.

Most of all, Mother wanted to feel safe. After all, she had three daughters to raise and a husband to care for, and she wanted to do what was expected of her, whether that was participating in New York City society or her church group, "or even *just* the damn Junior League," according to Aunt Billie. Mother equated safe choices with happiness. But Aunt Billie said Mother never made truly happy choices.

I was in my mid-teens when Aunt Billie told me in her deep Southern drawl, "The world won't make you safe, Joanie. So you might as well choose." She told me that life is all about choosing where and how to belong, that you couldn't *just* belong. I remember she paused a moment, then added, "Well, I mean you can 'just belong,' but it's about taking a risk, making it your choice, not following some foolish rule book."

Billie didn't like rules; they made her claustrophobic, she told me. She was different from Mother, whose life seemed to be governed by the Magnolia Code.

"But you have to know there's always a price to pay," Billie instructed. I can hear her stressing the words *price to pay* as she gave me her serious look. "Remember there are consequences to one's choices, or non-choices," she said. "But in the end, life's a bit of a dance," she said lightly, "so you might as well be yourself, 'cause everyone else is already taken."

I knew there was something right about Billie's attitude, her dare to be herself. I liked the idea that life's a dance, but of course at the time I wasn't sure what she meant. Now I know from experience that Aunt Billie was right; she was especially right about Mother, who had made her choice but wasn't prepared for the "price to pay."

Sometimes Mother seemed trapped—she walked fast, even in the apartment, always busy, like she was looking for something, or as if she needed to

Mother and I

find the exit. My sister Alicia once commented with a smirk that maybe Mother was looking for herself—just not in the right places.

The world outside the family apartment suited Mother better. She seldom lunched with friends but instead wandered New York, visiting thrift stores where one could find a bargain, and looking for pretty things in antique stores and the big auction houses. She loved the subway and the bus, and she enjoyed speaking to people wherever and whenever she had an opportunity. She did volunteer work at the church at least once a week. She hardly stayed at home in the daytime. There was no reason to, really, as Nanny and Sophie took care of us children.

Mother was pulled in two different directions. She had one foot in her Southern roots, in the lovely slow-moving town of Corwith, North Carolina, and one foot in the fast-paced, cosmopolitan Yankee bastion of New York—a city she loved but in which she was not the center of attention, no longer "Corwith's beautiful belle," as one of her boyfriends had written in her 1923 high school yearbook.

If she had stayed in the South, would she have continued to receive that adoration, or would it have waned with her youth? She left the South to follow Father into their life's adventure, but as she gradually lost him to his work and other women, she, in turn, began to lose her self-confidence and her ability to concentrate.

Mother didn't usually allow me the choice of a lunch place, or to have lunch at all—we were too busy to stop—but today was different because she had lost me, then found me. So now she turned her focus on me, the six-year-old who wanted to be part of her world. As we walked, I held onto her sleeve.

I told her I wanted to go to Horn & Hardart Automat on 57th Street and 6th Avenue. I knew how to slide my tray along the rail, deposit twenty-five cents in the slot under the picture of my favorite sandwich (always tuna fish), then open the plastic door and retrieve my meal. For another bit of change a soda or a slice of pie could be had, but Mother didn't like Horn & Hardart's pies. So for dessert we walked back over to the East Side to Schrafft's and sat at the counter. I asked for my usual ice cream sundae—coffee ice cream with marshmallow and caramel sauces topped with almonds. The restaurant served the ice cream in little silver cups that I stared at, waiting for them to frost. After she ordered cherry pie with a scoop of vanilla, Mother told me about the Irish secretaries who had followed us in for lunch.

"They look so nice in their suits, don't they? And they have red hair, just like your sister and father. They like to have fun, always laughing," she said, watching them pull together chairs, crowding a table. "They drink Manhattans," she added knowingly.

"What's that?" I asked. "Manhattan, that's where we live."

"Yes, we do, we live in Manhattan. Do you know it's an island? Long and narrow, like this," she said as she stretched out her hands. "The Manhattan drink, well, let's see. It's a mix of bitters, orange and bourbon, maybe vermouth, I think. Oh yes, and maybe sherry. Too sweet for me."

"What do you like to drink?" I asked.

Mother concentrated on her pie and replied, "Oh, I like a Dubonnet — just one or two a night—sometimes a glass of wine, but your father doesn't like serving wine. 'Too uptown,' he says." Mother laughed at the thought, and then told me stories of Irish New Yorkers and their hard times—how the British had mistreated them in Ireland, and that's why they came to New York so long ago. She knew tidbits like that and liked to share them, but my constant question, "What do you mean?" was rarely answered.

After the ice cream, I wanted to go to the nearby FAO Schwarz Toys, but Mother didn't want to. She said it would be too crowded, especially just before the holidays.

"But I want to see the fire engines."

"No, that's not a good idea today."

Every Christmas my parents allowed Alicia and me to pick out one toy each at Schwarz and include the wish for it in our letters to Santa Claus. For several years I had asked for the same toy: a fire engine, one I could pedal around our apartment. I drew a picture of it, including a bell, two ladders, and a hose, and mailed my letter a few weeks before Christmas. Santa Claus never granted my wish. Mother said Santa told her the apartment was too small for me to drive a fire engine in it. I wonder now why Father didn't write a letter, pretending to be Santa. He liked doing things like that on Christmas Eve—putting out milk and a sandwich by the fireplace. In the morning the sandwich was gone and the scrunched-up napkin had black soot on it.

So instead of the toy store, Mother and I walked through the lobby of the Plaza Hotel to visit the Palm Court and listen to the afternoon band playing Cole Porter tunes for the suited and hatted ladies. Mother read me the menu at the restaurant's entrance: tea sandwiches made of watercress, smoked salmon, or finely chopped egg salad.

We looked at the people "arriving from everywhere," Mother said, "who knows where? Oh, I could live in a lobby like this."

"I hear a Southern voice," Mother said to a woman standing by her luggage. "You must be on a visit?"

"Yes," answered the woman. "And how nice of you to speak to us." They talked for a while about their hometowns and what they were doing in the city. Mother told the woman that she missed her Southern friends, but added, "You can't beat the excitement of New York."

On the way home we stopped at Mother's church to tell the secretary when she would be coming in to volunteer for the Old Ladies Home around the corner.

"Why is it called that name? That doesn't sound nice," I asked.

"Well, that's who they are—lovely old ladies—and I like helping them," Mother replied. "I take them places. It's fun. Sometimes."

We climbed to the top of the bright red double-decker bus to return uptown to our apartment.

"Don't stare, but tell me what you think of people's hats," she whispered, then laughed.

"You stare, why can't I?"

"Joanie, sometimes it's impossible to answer all your questions," she said, now exasperated. "Just once in a while, don't ask."

3

Safety

Our apartment's front door opened into the foyer, a large square space that could have been an anchor for the rooms funneling off in each direction. Neutral territory, a crossroads, the foyer saw our comings and goings. One would think the space served to connect our flow, but it didn't. Instead it separated the tension-filled home. While all of us—including Nanny and Sophie—paid homage to the notion of "family," in fact we were individual beings acting out our identities, each in our solitary space.

Nanny and Sophie had arrived separately in the United States in the late 1930s. Although they were from different parts of Germany and had disparate personalities, they nevertheless became friends, partly out of the necessity to keep their part of our house calm and in working order, and partly because they shared a background that, by the end of World War II, subjected them to prejudice. Their voices were very different—Sophie spoke softly, while Nanny's speech had a rumble, lower and louder. Sophie was shorter, "a little more plump," she once confessed, acknowledging Nanny's more distinct figure. I never saw them upset with each other, but they sometimes shook their heads and said, "We didn't grow up the same way." They didn't explain what that meant, yet they were both sure of one thing: Germany was a place you wanted to leave.

"We dreamed of New York," they both said.

They told Alicia and me that although they previously had good jobs, caring for nice families and sweet children, we were their favorites.

The soul of our apartment lived in the kitchen. It was a refuge for us children. On winter school mornings I'd get up and hurry to escape the damp city cold that had sneaked through the cracked-open window into my bedroom. I'd quick, quick, put on my uniform and socks, find the brown Oxford shoes underneath my bed, and run to where Sophie was making hot chocolate. The kitchen was Sophie's domain. She usually stood by the oven with a readied wooden spoon in her hand. Her apron held the good kitchen smells.

Sophie met her husband in 1942, and they bought an apartment in the Bronx just two years before he died. She didn't talk about him much, but when she said she missed him, she pressed the tight gold band on her left ring finger. Age, weight gain, plus a bit of flour and grease caught up under the band made her ring dig deep. She said that no amount of butter was going to make it easy to slide off. But, she added, the occasional pinch of the ring reminded her of her husband. They didn't have children, so after he died, she came to live with our family.

At breakfast I sat catty-corner to Alicia. We were always poised to have the giggles, with Sophie egging us on. Never in a hurry or impatient, Sophie genuinely wanted to be with us. She puttered, hummed a German tune, and gave us a squeeze along with hot cereal. Her hairpins couldn't quite contain all the strands of hair in the bun on the back of her head, and inevitably a few pins would fall out onto the table. The clinking pins supplied us with more giggles. But if my parents were around, she'd be embarrassed.

Sophie and Mother got along well, finding common ground in talking about food and our evening guests.

"The Thompsons are coming over for dinner tomorrow. They like your veal. Please do that, Sophie, with your good sauce. Pour some of that Marsala wine over everything. You know I don't like Marsala much, but that does make it good."

"What about prune cake for dessert?" Sophie asked. "Dr. Thompson likes that, I remember. He said so the last time—after he dropped most of it on the floor." Sophie and Mother laughed.

"Oh, yes, poor thing, poor Sam, he did do that," Mother said. "That was awful, but we did laugh afterwards, remember, Sophie?"

For us, Sophie's connection to the "outer world," as she called it, held a fascination. She spoke of the "good spirits" found everywhere, which explained why she often left the back door ajar, just in case one was lurking. She mixed stories of these spirits into her fairy tales when she read our fortunes from the dregs of the hot chocolate cups.

"The princess was lost in the forest, and was saved by a frog," began a tale she described with enthusiasm the morning after Mother lost me in Best & Co.

Sophie

"I must be a princess," I said out loud. Sophie said yes, but Alicia reminded me that of course I wasn't—I was just a little girl.

I didn't know until years later how deep Sophie's penchant for interpreting dreams was. Alicia and I had left for boarding school and life was lonely in the apartment without us. Mother and Sophie found solace in each other and liked talking about their childhood memories and dreams. The vision of the two of them connecting in the safety of the kitchen produces a sweet yet surprising picture for me, as I never thought of Mother as a person who connected to "the spirits."

Thursdays and Sunday afternoons were Nanny and Sophie's days off. The kitchen was always left so tidy that Alicia and I were secretly afraid they wouldn't return. Without their energy the space felt dreary. The room's one window looked out onto our building's interior courtyard, a gloomy place typical of

New York apartment buildings. The window looked black because so little light was let in. Everything echoed in the courtyard. Milk bottles rattled in their metal crates as they were carried by the milkman through the back entrance and up the service elevator to the appropriate doors. The odd man who was the knife sharpener stood in the middle of the courtyard, singing up to all the surrounding apartments, "Bring down your knives, I'll do them right, sharp and right." Those may have been the only days Sophie opened the window wide, shouting back that she would straightaway be coming down with her cutlery.

I heard a story about people in another apartment who were moving away from New York. Their last night's dinner party over, they bid the city and their apartment farewell by throwing their dishes out into the courtyard and slamming the kitchen window shut behind them. I knew it wasn't a nice thing to do, but still, I thought it was funny.

Nanny

The nights my parents were out in the city—which were many—Alicia and I had dinner with Nanny and Sophie at the Formica kitchen table with its yellow checkered tablecloth. We liked Sophie's simpler, less formal cooking: string beans boiled in milk, crispy fried chicken, sausages and strudels that she brought home from the nearby German neighborhood of Yorkville. Alicia and I didn't want to be sitting properly at the dining room table with our parents. I didn't like the gamey taste of the pheasant or quail Father had recently shot, and I felt a sorrow for the tiny dead birds. And Mother took so long—she pushed her food around the plate as if she couldn't decide what to eat next. She said it was polite for her to be the last to finish.

Sophie moved quietly in and out of the dining room serving dinner. After cleaning the kitchen, she went back to her bedroom—bleak, small, and to me, lonesome—at the back of the apartment. A single bed hugged one wall, a junky sink jutted out of the opposite wall, and a half-sized tub and a toilet completed her living space. A small faded photograph of rural Germany—a house with a big family barely visible in the background—sat on the little bureau. We pointed to where Sophie stood in the family line and tried to remember the names of her brothers and sisters. She would nod with a smile and change the subject. From this joyless room, she could look out onto the same courtyard seen from the kitchen—which offered no sun, no light, and no sense of the day's weather unless it was raining or snowing pretty hard. But Sophie never complained.

Nanny arrived at our apartment soon after my birth at New York Hospital in 1944. Most people referred to her as our governess. Her real name was Anna Hofmann.

We slept in the same room. Because I loved her so much, I liked sharing our room. I never thought about her lack of privacy, which she really only found in the bathroom off our bedroom. With the door ajar, I could see the right side of her figure sitting on the lidded toilet. The black-and-white hexagonal floor tiles so ubiquitous in the city showed off her white uniform shoes, her crossed ankles. I could barely make out her quiet voice as she prayed the rosary, her head bent over her beads.

I watched this mystery from my bed each night. The rosary took about twenty minutes, and when Nanny finished, she opened the door next to the toilet—the closet that was filled with boxes of tissues, soaps, towels, and her large important sewing kit—and carefully returned her beads there until the next day.

Nanny showed me a picture of her big house and flourishing garden in Germany. She told me stories of her childhood as one of twelve children growing up outside a city called Munich, but she didn't go into the details of her family. She just said, "Oh, all of that—the house, the beautiful countryside—it's all gone." Someday, she said, she longed for a house by a little stream in the woods like the one near her childhood home.

I remember Nanny absent-mindedly picking up twigs in Central Park.

"Why do you do that?" I asked.

"Oh, it's a habit. During the war we didn't have heat, so the children had to find branches, anything to start a fire, to keep us warm."

"Were you very cold?"

"Yes, very cold, and we were hungry. Now, come on, let's go."

I wish I'd asked her more. "What were your parents like? What kind of fun did you have with your brothers and sisters? Did you like your school?" But I didn't.

Neither did I ask about the words she said to the beads. What did they mean? She didn't talk much about her Catholic faith, except for stories about the Maryknoll Sisters, who were missionaries. She wanted to be one of them. She went to church often, sometimes just to light a candle or to sit quietly for a time, she told me.

Nanny made her own clothes, mostly suits; they were plain, boxy, sturdy. She wore a white blouse underneath the jacket with a pin for decoration on the collar. She put her grey hair up in an old-fashioned style, and when her hair hung down, she looked scary, like a witch. I told her that and she laughed.

"Miss Hofmann is very correct," Mother once said to me. "Those are nice suits, but a little severe, don't you think, Joanie?"

I knew I couldn't take sides. "Oh, I don't know. They look nice to me, and anyway I don't know what 'severe' means."

Most mornings Nanny held our hands and walked Alicia and me to The Spence School, a few blocks from our home. Usually she picked me up in the afternoon, but not Alicia; at nine years old, Alicia could walk home on her own. At the end of the day, the school's downstairs hall would be crowded with waiting nannies. A low hum of German- and Irish-accented chatter filled the room. They stood straight and tall in their lace-up shoes, their hands folded in front of them, their hair pinned back.

But one afternoon, I spied Mother waiting in the crowd of nanny-grey uniforms, wearing a green-and-beige plaid suit and feathered crimson hat that brightened the scene. I ran to her, excited at the unexpected visit. I wanted her to be as happy to see me as I was to see her. I wanted to show her off: Look, Mother has come to pick me up. The scent of the perfume she called "Joy" surrounded me as I reached up for a hug, although I knew she wasn't much of a hugger.

"Look who came with me," she said. "It's your doll, Bertha. I wheeled her over from home in your little carriage."

I gasped at the surprise. I peeked up at Mother, suspicious at this unusually kind gesture. But I looked inside the brown rattan carriage and there was Bertha, reclining on a white pillow, dressed in pink with green leaves on her collar. It was Bertha's favorite dress. My plastic yellow purse sat propped next to her. The handkerchief inside was embroidered with "Joanie," just like Mother's, except hers bore her initials, AYB.

We walked a block to Central Park's 90th Street entrance.

"Why does Nanny always pick me up from school? Why don't you?"

Mother answered that she had things to do and Nanny often wanted to pick me up. "Perhaps she thinks it's her job," Mother added, as if it were an afterthought.

"Do you like Nanny?" I dared to ask.

"Why would you ask that? Yes, of course." She paused. "But sometimes she's stern, and takes you children with her when I want to be with you." She paused. "Why, do you think Nanny doesn't like me?"

I didn't think Mother and Nanny liked each other much, but I didn't know how to answer her. I just reached for her hand as we pushed Bertha's carriage to the park.

Years later, I wondered about her question. I was too young to understand the complexity of relationships, but I knew I felt safe with Nanny, while Mother's moods scared me.

The next school day, I half-hoped Mother would be waiting, but when the bell rang, Nanny stood in the hall and I ran to her. On our walk home, we passed St. Thomas More Church on 89th Street and Nanny suggested we go in for a minute. As I waited for her to say her prayers, I wandered off. A priest came up to me and asked, "Little, girl, are you waiting for confession?" I looked up at him in his big black dress and screamed, "Nanny, Nanny," and ran through the small church looking for her safety. The startled glances of worshippers followed me, but I didn't care.

"Who's that man, he scares me," I said, pointing down the aisle at the priest. With a frown on her face, Nanny rushed me out to the street. She took my hand, started giggling, and told me that the priest was part of heaven, and that one day when I went to heaven, I could have all the Popsicles I wanted.

I tagged along with Nanny whenever she would let me, especially on her errands in Germantown streets. Big sausages hung outside the meat store next to the Old Heidelberg Café. Candy and ice cream stores lined York Avenue. We crossed wide, bustling 86th Street, full of honking cars and accordion music booming out of the shop doorways, as we headed for Wankel's Hardware, the place she could go to fill a box with boots, coffee, tools, and whatever else her brothers and sisters, still in Germany, needed. The strong scent of brewing coffee and the aroma of cut wood from the boards leaning against the walls made me dizzy. While Nanny figured out the complicated mailing and talked to other Germans, I walked down the aisles imagining the needs of her family. I touched the strange-looking tools that twirled and measured and could break things apart, and I let the cool nails and screws slip through my fingers as they clanked into the hanging scale. The world in there, busy with buying, packaging, talk of other places—all in the sounds and rhythms of diverse languages—held an exotic mystery, and I stood waiting near the customers to listen and stare. Even at seven, I was already fascinated by the world "out there." One time Mr. Wankel—or the man I thought was Mr. Wankel—let me tape up a box. He told me, with Nanny translating, that I was a good girl. I was used to people barking at me to stop running, go sit down, wait over there. But on that day in Nanny's world, I was accepted and belonged.

She spoke German with her friends who came to our apartment, of course. Nanny and Fräulein Rock sat by our bedroom window and slipped into their shared old world. I heard foreign words and quiet laughter. Only sometimes did Nanny answer my badgering for a translation.

It could have been an opportunity for me to learn another language, but Mother said no, the language to learn would not be German, but French. I heard mean words about the Germans at my parents' parties. I didn't know the word "kraut," but I knew that Aunt Billie said it in an unkind way.

The harsh prejudice against the Germans in the 1950s was rampant and generalized. The war had recently ended, and the damage to lives, relationships and places impacted both Europe and America. But when I hear Germans being maligned today, my response is defensive. My German Nanny could do no wrong and I loved her as a mother. More than my parents, she created my sense of safety.

I have a memory about Nanny that disturbs me even now. As I lay in bed one night at a young age, Nanny said she wanted to teach me the Lord's Prayer. When she started to recite the prayer, I mistook the foreign-sounding words and phrases—which were Latin, of course—for German, and I responded defiantly, "No, that's German, Mother said I'm not supposed to learn that."

Nanny may have answered; I don't recall. I watched her get up from the side of my bed and walk slowly into the bathroom, quietly but firmly closing the door behind her. I imagined her sitting on the toilet lid, taking her rosary out of the closet.

After I left for boarding school at fourteen, returning for holidays and summers, I was happier to see Nanny and Sophie than I was to see my parents. I took for granted that my two guardians would always be there.

I didn't then realize that Mother was just as emotionally dependent on Sophie as I was.

On one of my trips home in my twenties, my mother recounted a dream she had shared with Sophie:

I was little and was wearing a blue taffeta dress with a big bow. On my feet were my new shiny black shoes with white socks. I had been told to go outside to play at my cousin's house but not to go far, as I was in my

Sunday-best dress. I saw a barn at the end of the magnolia bushes. That barn was what my parents meant by "too far," but I had to go see. I ran along the bushes, my hands sweeping the flowers in order to bring up the scent. The closer I came to the barn, the better the smell, a mix of magnolias and manure.

It was dark inside the barn. I couldn't see well, but I heard a stumbling and a low snort coming from a stall. My eyes adjusted to a shaft of that intense mid-day Southern light as it shone on a small pony, just a little bit taller than me. The pony came over, put his nose right up next to my neck. He wanted to be with me, I was sure. I found a stool and got up on his back, opened the latch on the gate, but the pony stumbled again and threw me down, ripping my dress.

"I was excited to tell Sophie that dream," Mother said to me. "She would have known exactly what it meant. You know she had an old-timey knowledge. It reminded me of my Southern roots, all that black wisdom we grew up with," she said, looking at me, putting her hand to her cheek in a dreamy way. Mother told me how she hurried down the hall to Sophie's room the morning after her dream.

"I knocked and opened the door slightly and looked in, just like I usually did. All was so quiet. Sophie seemed to be staring off in the distance, but she wasn't staring off at all. She had died."

I can still see Mother's lost look. She seemed so alone. Despite my own sadness, I was struck by the depth of her close bond with Sophie; maybe she was the only person Mother could talk to. I've since thought about how she defied her parents in that dream. When did she start following the rules? When did she start believing in the Magnolia Code?

Mother's relationship with Nanny was much different than her relationship with Sophie. It was detached. In the South, many mothers dismiss their nannies when a child is still quite young so the bond will diminish. But our Nanny stayed, returning to Germany only when I was in my late teens. I visited her in her village outside Munich when I was twenty-one and studying in Italy. One of her sisters picked me up at the rail station and drove me to their house, where Nanny stood outside in line with her two other sisters, all ready to welcome me. Nanny was proper, so I was surprised to see her dressed in a warm wool bathrobe in the afternoon. But her presence was the same: straight and tall, her hair up in her usual bun in the back, her hands folded in front of her. I threw my arms around her and rushed to tell her my excited feelings. She looked at me with a beaming face, but I soon realized she had lost her English.

I hadn't been told that she'd had a stroke.

She stared at me, struggling to find her words, tightly holding onto my arm.

I started to cry. I didn't want to. I didn't want her to know I was overwhelmed with sadness that she wasn't the Nanny I remembered, that I was too vulnerable in my need to connect with her.

The next day we took a slow walk. Starting to cry again, I told her I had to leave early. She looked at me and stammered phrases of German I couldn't understand, but I knew she was asking me why.

I have always felt a deep remorse that I couldn't rise to the occasion. I now realize that my uncontrollable tears came not just from sadness, but from the confusion of knowing I loved her more than I should have. In a way I loved her more than my own mother. Mother probably knew that. I feel a lasting sorrow for Mother's inability to find a place where she belonged. Instead she seemed lost, unmoored in her unsafe mothering sea.

4

Nick and Charlene's

Father had the run of most of the apartment while Mother, in a way, had none. She had no room to call her very own. The cook was in the kitchen, the three children had their bedrooms, and the living room—a fairly stiff space with couches, portraits on the wall, and dried flower arrangements on the tables— was dedicated to evening cocktail formality. Father made fun of what he called "your mother's private desk," the not-to-be-disturbed terrain next to the left side of her bed. There she dropped the messages she wrote to herself—scribbled bits of information on little pieces of paper—sometimes stepping on them when she got in and out of bed. The area could remain unruly, she said; it was her private place, and that was that.

Although light filtered into their bedroom from both Park Avenue and 90th Street, making it seem bright, the room had a grey cast. Nothing really stood out among the two lone beds, the two bureaus, the two doors into separate bathrooms, or the two closets. I didn't like being in their bedroom. It felt lonely.

Mother's bureau stood in the left corner. About four feet wide, it had two rows of drawers with gold-gilded handles and paintings of green leaves over a dull brown color. Scattered about on its surface were silver-handled hairbrushes, little treasure boxes, a stray pin or two, notes looking for a home. I remember it not because of the clutter but because of the allure of what lay underneath: photographs of people, mostly from the 1920s and '30s, their faded images stuffed carelessly in between the bureau and its glass top; more were stuck in the side edges of the gilt-framed mirror above. At age seven, I recognized only a few of the people in the old photos. I asked Mother, "Who's that? Where's that?"

I liked the slow, soft lilt of her accent when she dreamily answered, "Oh, he was an old friend, Lordy, I just heard he's dead." She pointed to another one. "My roommate at school; so pretty, isn't she, Joanie?" Or, "I've told you before about my old beau; here's the picture of him. I liked him especially. His name was Peanut." Her voice fell to a whisper. "I wonder where he is now."

"Tell me more about Peanut," I said. "That's a funny name."

She smiled and turned to gaze out the window.

"Oh, Joanie, you don't want to know, it's so long ago. And your father might come in; he always makes fun of Peanut. I better not tell you now. But someday, yes, I'll tell you someday."

She leaned down to look at the photo of Peanut, whose appearance was old-fashioned, his auburn hair parted in the middle. Standing up straight, she glanced in the mirror and picked up her tube of Revlon's red "Fire and Ice" lipstick, popularized in 1952 in ads that suggested a woman could be naughty *and* nice. She carefully colored her lips, then rubbed them together in that funny way. I looked at her straight nose. It seemed long to Alicia and me. She pointed to another old image, this one of her and her mother.

"Look at us sitting there, enjoying that Cuban warmth. I think we were drinking Cuba Libres."

"What's that?"

"Rum and Coca-Cola with lime juice. I remember the music; so good, so romantic. I wonder what we were thinking; can't tell from the picture, that's for sure. I liked Cuba but your father never really forgave me for going. We were just married and he only made $11 a week. Depression time, you know. You know about the Depression, Joanie?"

She didn't give me time to answer but continued looking at the picture of her mother and her.

"I shouldn't have gone and left your father at that time, but Mother told me I just had to go, that we'd have fun together. Well, Joanie, I was obliged to go, really. She wasn't well, had cancer. And thank heavens I did; she died soon after. We did have a bit of fun, but—" she hesitated—"really, your father should have been the one to travel with her. My mother and your father, they laughed a lot together; they were more alike than she and I. Oh well, that's in the past now."

As a child listening to Mother's talk—really more of a rambling to herself—I couldn't grasp her meaning. Today, as an adult, I realize that she told this story, like a handful of others she shared, seeking confirmation that she'd done the right thing. She had no one else to ask. But how could I, just a child, answer such a question?

I wondered why there weren't more pictures of us, her family—our birthday parties, or picnicking on the Fourth of July. Photographs of us blowing out candles, sliding down the rocks at Margaret's Falls. Those photos could have been put under the bureau glass. As I listened to her stories about people, I had a feeling that I didn't want to have, that she wasn't just my mother—that she was other people, too. She wasn't just for me, or for my sisters, or even for my father. All those pictures told stories about her world, a world I didn't know.

I stood next to her in front of the mirror to see if we looked alike, to see how tall I looked in comparison to her, and I saw a tear running down her cheek.

"Are you crying because you're thinking about Peanut?"

She pulled a handkerchief from her sweater sleeve and dabbed at her eyes.

"It was just something I was remembering. Oh, Silly"—she called me that sometimes—"don't bother with all that."

I wondered if Mother's mother had a special name for her, or if she had put out pictures of her children. I didn't ask. I didn't want Mother to cry again.

"Come on with me, we'll go make some fun," she said. "We have to. We'll go out, down on the streets where the fun is."

With the thought of joining the street's energy, Mother became someone else, someone I now recognize, because I have some of her and that street energy in me. It meant engagement with the city, away from the limits of the apartment.

She put on her warm green jacket with the braid on the sides and looked for her hat. She adored berets, "like the French," she told us, but this beret had a feather in it—"something extra." After a few hellos with our doorman, she

Three sisters

began walking fast, away from Park Avenue. "It's dull there, no windows to look at." On Lexington we smelled the newly baked foods coming from the German bakeries. Mother said hello to the Chinese laundryman. Father had given him some pheasants he had shot last weekend. "Let's ask Mr. Chung if he liked them.

"From there we'll go to Nick and Charlene's. I need a laugh. We'll see what beautiful things they've found to sell. Come on, you like them," she said. I always wanted to be with her on her antique shopping walks or her search for old jewelry in the booths of the West 40s and Ninth Avenue. She knew those places, could tell her friends where to go, whom to ask for, to find the good buys. The vendors liked her and called her by her first name, Alice, not the formal "Mrs. Baker" most everyone else called her.

We walked down the few steps into the small antique store on East 77th Street. Nick and Charlene's wasn't junky and crammed like other stores I'd been in with Mother, places where you could easily break something. Theirs was crowded, but chairs hung on the walls with mirrors next to them; a table was set with fancy knives and forks and old napkins with initials. Mother always went over to the collection of blue-and-white vases.

They greeted us with enthusiasm, and then asked me a few questions about first grade, but they were more interested in sharing stories of the ways of buyers and sellers, the bargaining tricks people used to get a better price, and then they all laughed.

I sat in an overstuffed chair in the corner to watch and listen to the three of them discuss the new pieces, furniture, and china. Mother giggled when she overheard Nick's conversations on the back-wall pay telephone as he spoke to his horseracing people. Nick, a big man with a Bronx accent—one he said came from his "tough-guy days"—teased her about being Southern.

"Alice, where in tarnation is Dixie?"

I saw her wink at Nick and answer in a slow Southern drawl, "Oh, just a little ol' place down South. But you Yankees watch out, I'm not just a country girl. I like being Southern, but don't you believe I don't know how to get around this big city."

Winking wasn't like Mother. She laughed a lot with strangers, but mostly she remained slightly aloof. I don't think anyone would have put their arm around her the way Father put his arm around people. But with Nick and Char, she became more sure of herself and enlivened by their easy conversation and shared knowledge. Father loved beauty, but he didn't place much importance on the fine things that Mother cared about. I watched her swoop around, picking up objects, giving her opinion on the value or history of pieces. She probably forgot I was there.

"Oh, I've heard things about that place called Dixie, how those small towns—like your town you talk about—are beautiful and friendly." Nick paused. "Not sure I'd want to be a colored person down there though, even today."

"No, maybe not," she answered, "but in my family, we treated our help well."

Just then the shop doorbell rang as a customer walked in, interrupting Mother's proud explanation of her family's Southern manners.

Nick encouraged Mother to speak with the customers.

"You know stuff, you know value, and, Alice, you're so ladylike, you dress nice, people might think this is a swell place!" he teased her. I watched Nick and Char exchange glances. When the customer left, Charlene came over to Mother.

"Alice, we've been thinking. This may sound crazy, but what would you think of this idea? Why not work here with us?" Charlene hesitated, waiting for Mother's reaction. She started up again with a hurried voice, "Seriously, why not? Let's say twice a week or whatever you can manage."

Nick came over with a big smile on his face.

"We could put all our knowledge together. And we'll do a trade with you for whatever you would want. What do you say? It doesn't have to be rigid. No, not at all. Come on, you Southern belle, we'd have fun." Nick laughed.

Mother paused. She had put down the old scratched mirror she'd been examining as she listened intently to their offer. She distracted herself by pulling out her handkerchief from her sweater sleeve.

The memory of that moment remains vivid. I can see you, Mother. I can see your face turning into a wide smile as you looked from Charlene to Nick.

"What, what are you saying? You would want me to work with you?" You walked toward them with a surprised and happy look, especially when Nick said something about a good horse race, and you all laughed.

But then I saw you change; a change came across your face, as if you had thought of something sad.

"You know, it's just where I'd like to be," you said. "Oh, Lordy, what fun we would have." You turned and looked at me, suddenly remembering that I sat in the chair nearby. "Let me think about it. I'd better talk to my husband; I don't know, he's very Southern in his ways so, you know … he might think I should be doing things at home."

"Nobody's funnier about their ways than my big Italian man," announced Charlene. "Yes, just rest on it, Alice."

Nick and Charlene seemed to understand Mother.

Preoccupied on our walk home, Mother became irritated and pulled on my arm to cross the street.

"Okay, Joanie, I'm sorry, but we'll have to go faster. I have to think about this idea, maybe talk to your father tonight."

I quickened my step.

But as usual, the fun was over when we arrived home. She snapped at me to do my homework.

"First graders don't have homework," I said. I found Alicia, and we played in my bedroom, out of the way.

Mother had forgotten that out-of-towners, people connected to Father's firm on Wall Street, were coming for cocktails. She tried to make hors d'oeuvres with Sophie—some kind of cheese with chutney.

"Sophie, please pull out the frozen shrimp."

"Oh, Mrs. Baker, I hope these will un-freeze in time."

"Heavens above, they have to. And while you're in the freezer, see if you can find the cigarettes in that cellophane package. They should still be pretty good. I'll put them in the little silver vase in the living room."

Father came into the apartment in a rush, a bunch of cut flowers in his arms. He called out, "Joanie, get out the ice. Alicia, start up the Player Piano." Irritated, he added, "Hurry up, Alice, this is important to me."

Mother wouldn't bring up the subject of Nick and Charlene that night, like she said she would. Nobody was in a good mood.

The next morning I heard her on the telephone telling Mrs. Thompson of the offer. Mrs. Thompson must have said something encouraging as I heard Mother answer, "Maybe, yes, it could be a good idea. I do so like antiques. And, I do know something about them. But that husband of mine, well, I just don't know. He wants me to be more organized, spend more time at home.

"I'm just not good at that, Ruth." I heard her attempt a laugh.

When we'd visited Nick and Charlene's shop that day, Mother had a glimmer of hope, a chance that there was some other occupation for her. I wonder if she knew she could actually make the choice. I heard her voice falter on the phone.

"I know, Ruth, yes, I'm so lucky to have house help. I know, but there's always so much to plan. John's family is visiting this weekend and they want to be entertained every minute. And you know they never really like anything I've planned. Oh, Ruth, I'm going to have to think on this for a while … no, I won't think too long. Oh, Lordy, there's the doorbell. I'd best go."

She hung up the phone and hurried to the door, making clicking noises with her heels.

As far as I know, she never did bring up the subject with Father.

5

Cocktails

"Cactus, go make me that good drink the way I showed you. Pour a good inch or more of Johnnie Walker red. Remember the shaved ice. Throw in some soda, you know how. And let's have some music. Alicia, push that button on the Victrola, play the Cole Porter record I just bought."

At the age of eight, I was happy to be enlisted with the scotch-and-soda task. Alicia and I wanted to do as Father instructed.

As he settled into the chaise longue in his corner of the master bedroom, we would sit somewhere close, waiting for him to play with us.

"I loves you chirren. I do, I do. I loves you this much," he said, spreading his arms wide. "That's what my mother used to tell me," he reminisced. He told us again the story of how, at the age of twelve, he drove the family's old Studebaker from Jacksonville to Nova Scotia. "Can you imagine, it took us two solid weeks." Father laughed hard at the memory of his little sister, Miggie, who would want to have a pee beside the car. As soon as she was settled, he couldn't resist driving off. He imitated Miggie's squeals of horror.

Both of my parents grew up in an atmosphere of easy Southern cheer: good schools, church lessons, dating, picnics, and swimming in the river. They met at a dance while he was in college near Mother's small hometown, a beautiful North Carolina community of magnolia and azalea tree-lined streets. They married in 1929. The wedding was held in her family's very Southern nineteenth-century home on North Union Street. It was written up in the local society page. "Her dress was the epitome of fashion. The South is losing a favored daughter to the Yankees," the columnist asserted.

But the Depression was already on its way. As construction work hit a stand-still, my paternal grandfather's sand and gravel business in Jacksonville went bankrupt. Father's parents had not been able to afford a wedding gift, so they stamped Mother's new initials, AYB, on the back of their own silverware, and wrapped it up. I am reminded of their generosity as I use that silverware every day.

Father's family was religious. Their code of ethics emphasized service, duty to mankind, and honor to one's heritage. Although they saw themselves as Americans first, they believed in and belonged to that Southern class through which respectability and graciousness blessed them with superior traces of gentility. That slavery also marked the family history did not occur to them as shameful, but simply as part of their entitlement.

In keeping with the family values, the offspring were determined to pay back their father's debts from the economic collapse.

"That's what one did," Father explained with pride. All six children, three boys and three girls—young adults by 1932—were forced to choose new paths for their unsteady futures. My father chose New York City, where he proffered, with a façade of confidence, "I can make it there," long before Frank Sinatra recorded the emblematic song.

Young and determined, my parents arrived in the city exuding positive energy into Depression uncertainty. Armed with perseverance, gifts of charm, and a small bag of connections to other Southerners "gone North"—and armed, too, with white privilege and education, and a bit of money inherited from Mother's deceased father—their success was almost assured.

Father boasted that he had started at the bottom and pulled himself up. If he did use Mother's inheritance, he never mentioned it. His male pride would not have allowed that. In fact, I suspect he secretly resented her upbringing, which was more refined than his.

They were opposites in other ways. He had a positive streak, a face full of good nature, a golden boy. Mother's presence had a graciousness that expressed interest and curiosity, but not self-confidence. She asked caring questions, especially of those she met at church who came to our home for Sunday lunch.

"Tell me about your country, I'd like to know your culture," I heard her query a foreign student. To the new assistant minister, "I, too, am from a small town. Tell me about yours." Father did not ask questions; his goal was to make himself and others laugh, which he easily accomplished.

They must have looked like a winning couple. Their predicted success came to fruition and by the end of the '30s, Father had helped pay back his father's debts and was earning good money. Wall Street had again started to "boom," a word my father favored. My parents were beginning to be flush enough to afford to go dancing to the big bands, sometimes in Central Park, or even at The Stork Club. Prohibition had ended; they could now have a legal drink at Jack and Charlie's 21 Club.

Father was too old to enlist in World War II, but he knew that the Nazi danger had to be stopped, that if London fell, America could be next. His brother, wounded in Japan, wouldn't talk about the terrors of the fighting, but he did talk about courage, something Father valued.

In 1953 we were too little to understand Father's grown-up stories, but because he made his tales funny, we listened. He said we were the lucky ones, that many people still struggled to get back on their feet after the Depression and the war. He spoke of the war's good impacts: employment was up, the G.I. Bill benefitted the veterans. He hesitated a moment, and then added the not-so-positive impacts: he wasn't sure about America's new global position, nor too positive about Jackie Robinson crossing the baseball color line, and he didn't like President Truman.

"But look what happened, we won the war, just a year after you were born, Joanie, and everything is good now. Ain't life grand?" He tickled Alicia until she couldn't stand it. I never asked why they had waited so long to start a family; it wasn't until 1936 that Barrett was born, Alicia in 1942. I arrived in 1944.

Father's sense of fun covered up most of his worries, but I learned of his fastidious side in a recently discovered old checkbook register. Written in his distinct hand was a precise list: one carton of cigarettes, ten gallons of gas, a drink at The Plaza, a lock for his safe, a loan of $10 to a friend. Generosity was indicated by constant presents to family and friends. But his notation of these items helped me understand another side of him, and perhaps also to comprehend the era I was born into—that the prevailing mix of caution with a carefree positive attitude, both resulting from World War II weariness and Depression losses, strongly influenced the atmosphere of the times.

My parents' life was an uptown life, without the rush, he said, of the midtown publishing and advertising worlds, or the Bohemian madness of writers like Allen Ginsberg and Jack Kerouac, artists such as Jackson Pollock and Willem de Kooning, names he hardly knew or cared about. He lumped this mass of creative energy altogether as "downtown people." My parents had little interest in the arts. Certainly, they would go to a museum, a concert, the theater—always a musical—but only once in a while. When I finished college, the response given to my desire to become a photographer was, "There's really no money in the arts, Joanie."

I think of those early evenings when Alicia and I snuggled up to Father in his big chair, waiting for his hugs. He pointed to his upper arms, flexed his muscles, and asked with a low growl, "You remember what these two muscles mean?"

"Tell us again Daddy, what, what?" begged Alicia.

"Don't mess with me! This left muscle gives you seven days in the hospital; the right one spells sudden death." He threw back his head, but looked to see if we laughed with him.

"Oooooh, Daddy, do you mean it? Is it true?" we squealed. "Did you send someone to the hospital?"

"Well, no, but I should have. I've run into some pretty nasty characters who've come down from Harlem, other mean places."

"Why were they mean?"

"Oh, you know, not always nice people."

"Now show us, show us how you blow smoke out of your ears."

He took a long drag off his cigarette, cupped his hand, and—without looking like he was doing anything—made smoke magically wander over to his ear.

Our laughter slowed when Mother came into the bedroom. Unlike my father, she carried an awkward uneasiness. She wandered around restlessly, puttering with clothes, making lists of things, looking out the window—all the while whispering to herself. We knew she wanted to be part of the fun, or part of something, but she didn't know how to participate.

"Come on, girls, do your homework," she said to separate the three us. "John, we need to get dressed. People are arriving in an hour." Her gloomy mood affected all of us. We hoped she would find something else to do—somewhere else. Finally she left to putter in the kitchen.

"Okay, I'll get dressed," Father said, rising from his comfortable seat. "But you girls stay in here with me." We sat on his bed to watch his dressing ritual. He held two silver hairbrushes, one in each hand at the same time. Their soft bristles made me wonder how they made a dent getting through his fine red hair, which then was flattened down in an old-fashioned comb-over look.

He kept his shirts in two of the four drawers of his bureau, a slightly taller, thinner version of my mother's chest of drawers, but his locked with a key. Mostly white or blue, the shirts were folded with a cardboard in the middle, fresh from the Chinese laundry. Cufflinks sat on top of the bureau in a green leather case. Before he put on his suit pants, he arranged his garters to hold up his socks just so.

"Well, little girls," he asked, "what do you think of these?" snapping them loudly around his leg. "Gotta keep them purty silk socks straight, you know that, my little Cactus. Wouldn't want to trip over them."

He gave me a wink and hooked the silk socks to the garters, pulled up his neatly creased pants, and slipped his feet into polished lace-up shoes.

A multitude of ties hung from a rack on the back of his closet door. He chose carefully.

"Let's see, will tonight call for a subdued one? Or striped? Maybe decorated with birds or fish? What do you two think?" He met our eyes in the mirror and winked. "What will make me the prettiest man at the party?"

Handkerchiefs—all white, and embroidered JDB—were folded and neatly stacked in their own drawer. Placing his handkerchief was the last act of his performance. He opened the starched square, and arranged it in his suit jacket's top pocket to reveal just a little pyramid of white. One final look in the mirror and he was ready for the night's entertainment, wherever that might be.

Southern hospitality may have been in my parents' blood, but they also used it to distract themselves from quarreling. That particular night, after Alicia and I watched Father dress, they entertained just a few people at home for cocktails. When the group left, our dinner was ready, and the fight started. Fights usually began with a gesture, a word, a laugh at the wrong moment, or a suspicion.

"I suppose you're going to see Kent again after work tomorrow?"

"Yes, I must. He needs help with his financials."

"Why do you need to help people at the firm? They must have accountants to assist with personal work."

"Alice," Father answered, "why are you asking me these questions when you know I like to help people? And Kent is my friend."

We fidgeted. As children do, we thought their fights might be our fault, provoked by one of us doing something, anything. Sometimes Mother seemed to be spinning with irritation and we didn't know where her anger would land. We tried to learn how best to get out of the way and not wince when she told us to hurry up or slow down, all in the same breath.

In the tension of the dining room we were trapped. And we knew Father would soon say, "Oh, Alice, take a Miltown," the "calming pill" of that era. We knew his directive implied the argument was her fault.

But I remember that particular evening because Mother's suspicion—that the appointment with "Uncle" Kent was in reality going to be a quick flirtation with someone—proved true when Uncle Kent called the next night, looking to speak to Father. They hadn't coordinated their lie.

Aunt Billie, Mother's adopted sister, made cocktail parties fun. She had a short walk down the avenue from her apartment to ours. Always ready for the party to begin, she arrived a half-hour or so early in order to catch a few laughs with Father, knowing Mother was preparing in the kitchen. Billie had recently arrived in New York after her divorce from her latest husband, Francis. Father immediately had given her the nickname of "Billie Goat" and said she was going to "knock 'em dead." She liked the name Billie, liked it better than Willa, the name given to her by my grandmother. So in 1955 Billie discarded the old-fashioned Southern "Willa" and became Billie.

She entered the den where I was helping Father prepare the other bar ("Always provide two places to supply a drink," he told us. "Everyone needs a drink pretty fast") and threw her leopard-print coat over the chair. Billie's fashionable "poodle cut" accented her tightly curled hair and coordinated well with her wide skirt, appliquéed with cats. I remember how slim she was and that her two-inch heels brought her to the perfect height of 5'7". She had an easy way of moving through a room.

Stuffed birds, prints of hunting dogs and shooting scenes decorated the den's walls. A large case filled with shotguns stared at us from across the couch. Billie liked to tease Father, asking if he had stuck one of those guns out the window and bagged a few pigeons.

"Yes, I believe I did, and those were damn good shots." He grinned.

"That is some beautiful coat," Father remarked. "Where did that come from? But aren't you a little warm this evening? It's almost hot tonight."

The mean bitterness of the New York winter was over. That morning I had seen the gardeners starting to plant the first spring flowers in the Park Avenue median.

"Oh, John," Billie chuckled as she teased the coat's hem with her foot. "Francis gave it to me, and he just loved it so. He did have good taste. Maybe that's all he had," she winked. "I love this fabulous coat and I'm wishing for a cool enough Yankee spring. I wonder what that sister of mine will think? She'll tell me it's wrong, too flashy." She stretched her arm over the chair back and let her unlit cigarette dangle from her long, straight fingers, awaiting, I guessed, a light from Father. "To her I'm just a wild child who doesn't know diddle. Sometimes I wish we got along better, but Sis is too proper. Bet she'll look at me in this coat and think I'm her tacky sister come up to the big city. I can almost hear her."

"Maybe she's jealous. Maybe she wants your coat," Father said. They laughed. Father got up to "freshen" their scotches. He had told me the week before, after I asked Mrs. Thompson if she wanted another drink, to never say "another drink," but instead to use the term "freshen," or better yet ask, "Mrs. Thompson, may I make your drink more comfortable?"

I hoped Mother hadn't overheard the coat conversation. She was busying herself in the kitchen putting cheese on little pieces of toast, with the crust cut off—"just so," Billie said as she imitated Mother's cutting gesture. I bet Mother would want to drop one of those cheese toasts right on Billie's leopard coat.

It was easy to see that Father and Billie were pals. They amused each other, egged one another on. Father said he liked feistiness in a woman, but he warned Alicia and me that too much spunk was hard on a husband.

"And Billie's already had two of those," he declared in front of Billie. She laughed with him at that remark.

Years later, I wondered if Billie and Father could have been having an affair. They flirted and teased and sought each other's company. They had fun displaying their friendship overtly; she was his Billie Goat.

Billie worked part time for *Harper's Bazaar*, awaiting a promised full-time job in the magazine's copy department. Father asked how the job was going.

"I do love to work there, but I've learned not to ask anyone an important question after those three-martini lunches. No tellin' what answer you'll hear," she said in her drawl—similar to Mother's, but scratchier, full of smoke and scotch. "Big, exciting, creative, that's New York." She jiggled her glass; she liked to hear the ice clink. "Yes, the rest of the United States chokes from those proper values that came in with that Mr. Eisenhower. Thank God we live in the big city.

"Look at that, Joanie." She patted the space next to her on the couch for me to sit, as she opened a *Life* magazine sitting on the coffee table and pointed to an image on the first page that declared the 1950s the era of cigarettes and cocktails. "Let's celebrate, let's Live," proclaimed a scotch ad that displayed a blonde woman leaning against the Chrysler Building, one high-heeled foot peeking out from under a wide-striped skirt.

I sat next to her, eager to hear her funny comments and proud she wanted to share her thoughts. Billie said I'd understand things, not now, but in a few years—just as Isaiah had said.

"Joanie, it's best you know: those who want to express themselves, in writing, acting, music, or just plain good living without so many boundaries, well, they just come straight away to New York. But that wide-open expression of living big isn't necessarily celebrated on the Upper East Side, is it, Brother John?" She gave Father a smile and a nod. Billie complained about the proper way people behaved uptown, but she was quick to announce her thrill of being out of the stilted South. "I finally made it up to the real city."

"There's definitely glitter, just not a lot of combustion uptown," Father answered. "But life sure has become more fun since you came north, Billie." He leaned over to give her arm a squeeze. "You come over to see us anytime. Just don't bring that black cat of yours. Cats, they scare me to death. 'Spit in your hat when you see a black cat,' that's what I do.' "

"Oh, John, you're silly. Cats are powerful symbols of femininity—and that's the reason you men are afraid of them."

Billie's beloved black cat, Bastet, held a position of importance in her life. She didn't care that people were scared of cats, not even black ones. Instead she enjoyed recounting the story of Bastet, the cat goddess, companion to Isis, the ancient Egyptian deity. Since Bastet was known as the guardian against the evil spirits, Billie adopted her as her protector.

When Father left the room to fix the pantry bar, I asked Billie why she needed protection.

At that moment Billie rose from the couch and slowly waved her arms back and forth, calling out "swish, swish" in a far-off deep voice. Spurred on by the drink in hand, she made turns around the room, slowly twirling and twirling. She stopped and looked at me. "A while ago, Joanie, someone told me something that shook my world, a possible secret. So I sought out a Gypsy woman near my hometown who knew about the mysteries. She wasn't a witch but she understood the powers. Do you know what the powers are, Joanie?"

"No," I whispered.

Billie explained the powers. I remember the moment much more than her explanation, but I came to understand her story, as she told it many times through the years. She said that when you feel the powers, you have a connection to the earth's deep-down meaning.

"Powers are about the soul's connection, and above all the soul needs to feel good. I told the woman I wanted to put my confusion into a safe place, and that if I found that place, I would be okay, that somehow I would feel balanced."

I sat in the little rocker, my favorite chair, mesmerized. I was silent. I didn't understand—but I wanted to.

Aunt Billie

"The Gypsy woman told me I must own a cat, that I would find balance in the cat's tail, because the tail can hold the opposite energies—you know, like good and bad, light and dark, life's opposing paths. You've seen cats fall, Joanie; they always land on their feet, it's their tail correcting the fall on the way down. Balance for the soul, it's as simple as that," she said.

"And," she said, "the Gypsy woman told me something else you must remember: No one can own the cat, and I surely do like that thought."

She started to move again.

"See, watch me, Joanie, this is the cat's dance of the energies. And now, it's my dance." She imitated and swished her imaginary tail. Billie hummed and kept moving, turning.

Hearing Father's footsteps, Billie slowed her dance to a near stop.

Bastet

"Joanie, you understand even though you're still so young, and you like Bastet. Come play with her anytime."

Father caught Billie's last swirl. He smiled and stared at her while announcing that the guests were arriving.

"Come on, Billie, you be Alice for a moment, she's fixing in the kitchen."

I liked Billie's visits, especially at parties. I wasn't shy but hesitant. She watched out for me, pushing me in front of her, making people notice. Mother and Father liked Alicia and me to dress up, come out to say hello, but not take too long in returning to our rooms. But I always wanted to hang around with the guests, to weave my way through the chatter and the big laughs that swirled around the room, occasionally perching myself near someone friendly or who was maybe just bored with the nearest guest. I loved the sound of the ice clinking in the crystal glasses, the smell of cigarette smoke, the scent of good perfumes—especially one called Vivre. The women were nicer; the men didn't allow me much space. I learned to say things fast when I realized that grownups had short or no attention spans for my thoughts and, I noticed, for each other's thoughts as well, unless someone was telling a joke. My questions were answered by a nod, a pat on the head and a smile.

Someone usually sat at the piano playing a few tunes. Father wanted to play, but he said his stubby fingers couldn't reach an octave. We thought that wasn't true, that his mother told him only girls should play. So he invested in a piano that was also a self-playing one. We'd put in the song's roller and the keys magically depressed.

Mother moved around the room, serving the hors d'oeuvres, chatting, playing the interested hostess. At one point Father jokingly announced the next song would be for Alice. "It's called, *I Can't Get Started*." Everyone knew he was teasing Mother about getting things done, finishing the apartment. It wasn't the lyrics; it was the title that made people laugh. She pretended to go along with the joke until she saw him put his hand on Billie's shoulder and say in a loud whisper, "You know, Billie, the apartment's decorated in swatches."

Mother overhead the comment as she was meant to. She shot him a hurt look that he answered by pretending he was playing the violin, miming, *You always hurt the one you love*. I could see some of the guests staring at Mother's sad face. She didn't cry, never did cry, but stared at Father, her silver tray tipped at a slight angle in her hand.

Billie looked at Mother and finished her drink.

6

I Spy

People have asked if it was strange to grow up in New York. Strange? As a child I thought everyone grew up in New York. My world had ease, privilege and adventure, but my imagination was vivid and longed to cross boundaries into other lives, other territories. I was always on the lookout for a new path.

So at age eleven, I became a spy—mostly in my dreams. I had a recurring one: I stood outside a window and spied into a living room. Always in black and white and slightly blurry, the dream had an intensity to it. On waking I daydreamed, adding to the scene spine-cracked, broken-down books, their titles embossed in antique gold. I had recently seen a movie on "the Far East," so I placed a large book by that name on a beautiful table. Framed photographs atop a piano's threadbare shawl boasted days of fun, skiing, a family posing together, a bride in a wedding portrait. The shawl hung down in a haphazard fashion, similar to the Chinese one I now drape on my own piano. An opened letter lay by an envelope, a pen nearby, but I couldn't read the address.

In my fantasy I never put people in the room, yet I felt the warm atmosphere, along with my need to belong, pulling me inside. An opposite force kept me outside the window, a secret and safe observer.

We didn't have photographs of our family on display. On our den's walls hung prints of hunters shooting at flying things, or photographs of my father in Africa standing over dead animals, or holding a string of colorful birds. Neither were there any pictures of us in the living room. Above the couch hung a large portrait of one grandmother; from the opposite wall gazed the other grandmother, nearby a dark landscape. I once commented that all the photographs in the den had something dead in them.

From our apartment's fifth-floor windows—which offered views into the rooms of the building some twenty-five feet across narrow 90th Street—the spy in me kept watch. In the late afternoons a little boy sat at the piano for his hour-long practice sessions. His frustrated moans and banging of the keys traveled from his window to ours. Sometimes he threw his sheet music and I heard him crying. His mother came in and put her arms around him. From the Park Avenue windows of our apartment, I watched fast-moving crowds of people as they hurried to and from work; they let their minds wander and so bumped into each other. A man grabbed a woman's purse and ran down the street. In her high heels she chased him and knocked him down. People came to her aid. I yelled out the window, "Yay for you, yay, I saw you!" The woman looked up at me, surprised. Once a taxi screeched to a stop in front of a man who had slipped in the rain and lay on the street; some people ran to help, while some stood frozen. In the evenings I craned my neck for the nighttime show of women in evening dresses and top-hatted men, all waiting under the street lights for cars or cabs. I imagined the lives of all these people, their world outside our apartment.

Perhaps we all wanted to be somewhere else. Mother found her comfort on the streets; Father found his with someone other than Mother. I created my comfort in stories. The train leaves Grand Central Station at 42nd Street and travels uptown through Harlem and the Bronx on its journey north. Fifteen minutes after exiting the station, we pass within a few feet of an apartment building, close enough to my compartment window for a quick glimpse inside. A shade is pulled half down. Curtains, soiled grey from the constantly passing trains, are tied back from the opened window, giving the drooping avocado plants sitting on the sill a bit of air and sun. A hand reaches up to shut out the clackety-clack of the train. A silhouette. My moment's entry into another world.

A very real comfort was my school. By the time I was nine, I was allowed to walk the block and a half to Spence, but I actually ran across Park Avenue and over to Madison, slowing down to look into each shop window, then turning the corner onto 91st Street. The entrance to Spence wasn't formidable, just a double black door.

"Good morning, Nels. Fine, thank you, Nels," I greeted the kind but towering doorman with his thick Norwegian accent. We were taught to curtsy and shake hands and so we did, Nels extending his huge, white-gloved hand toward our small ones. He wore a double-breasted, brass-buttoned uniform jacket and brimmed cap. Black framed glasses topped his thin, straight nose. I liked his presence; he felt safe and was concerned for us.

We entered the school walking, not running, into the old-fashioned elegance of the foyer, where Miss McPherson, the school secretary, stood next to Miss Conklin, the somewhat stern head of school. They looked a bit alike—tall, slim women projecting welcome in their correct suits with nicely coiffed (but not stylish) grey hair. Miss McPherson seemed frail, but had a friendlier, more caring face than Miss Conklin, who maintained a proper façade. The students knew these two formal women were close friends. Years later I wondered if they were more intimately, if secretly, entwined. I hoped so.

The foyer's black-and-white parquet floor led to a winding staircase by the elevators. Once out of sight of Miss McPherson and Miss Conklin, we noisily jumped up the stairs two steps at a time to show our athletic prowess or, if feeling lazy, we took the elevator, operated by Elizabeth Rose, a petite young Irish woman. At the fourth floor she announced, "Okay, all you smart little girls, off you go, and you'd better learn something today. Come back and tell me."

I liked school, especially a teacher named Mrs. Sweeney. She spoke to us almost like adults and in third grade gave us a book to read, expressing in a simple way the meaning of justice in the world. I still remember my friend Debbie's father pronouncing the book Communist; he had it taken away from us. Mrs. Sweeney left the school soon after.

In the spring of 1955 I learned from a science teacher at Spence how to make a shoebox camera.

"Put a small hole in the front, then a pinhole in the back," she instructed. "Paint the interior of the box black and tape the edges." She gave an intricate description of how to put a metal piece over the hole, how—in a dark closet—to place the photo paper against the back side. Then she explained a simple development process. It was just what I wanted, the best possible spy tool.

"Go outside, look at the world, look at the details, take pictures," she told us.

I carried my camera everywhere. I now realize how much my snapshots—not only in childhood, with the shoebox and later, my Brownie camera, but now, with sophisticated equipment—have helped me to make sense of life from my own perspective.

Spence sat on a small piece of 91st Street and stood next to the massive Carnegie mansion, built at the turn of the century and occupying a quarter of a city block. It had been the time of the "robber barons," as Father called them. Its imposing wrought-iron gates—always closed—were alluring, daring me to enter. Someday, I told myself, I'll get inside.

And I did. One sunny afternoon, leaving the school for my two-block walk home, I saw the gate standing ajar. No one stood in the guardhouse. Timidly but quickly, my camera and I stepped in and headed toward an entanglement of paths, shrubs, shacks and sheds.

Nanny had read to me Frances Hodgson Burnett's book, *The Secret Garden*, about Mary Lennox, a little girl who found the key to a long-ago-locked garden. I often implored, "Read that part to me again."

It was the lock of the door which had been closed ten years and she put her hand in her pocket, drew out the key and found it fitted the keyhole. She put the key in and turned it.... Then she slipped through it, and shut it behind her, and stood with her back against it, looking about her and breathing quite fast with excitement, and wonder, and delight.

I was standing inside my own secret garden. I held Mary's key. I had entered the mystery of a hidden world. Gingerly I started down the narrow path, hoping to avoid any gardeners' eyes. I couldn't use the excuse of being lost, since I had knowingly trespassed. I had to hurry. The wintertime lack of foliage didn't provide many hiding places. I darted into a large shed that held shelves filled with books and packets of seeds—marjoram, sage, thyme.

Spring had just begun. Shears, rakes, bags of dirt, containers of new bulbs—all waiting for planting time—lay neatly against the lean-tos, covered by twisted branches. Cast grey cement benches decorated with carved cherubs and angels lined the paths. Fountains, now dry, awaited the return of birds. Romantic images of women and men sitting in old-fashioned dress sipping tea filled my imagination. I stepped quickly, lost in fantasy, occasionally pointing my camera at spots that caught the light and shadow of the crisscrossed branches.

Where are the gardeners? I wondered. I hoped for the best, and continued sneaking from shed to shed, bush to bush. Seeing a half-open glass door with clippers leaning on the step, I entered and tiptoed up the spiral staircase to the solarium's landing—the very room into which I had spied from my fourth-floor study-hall seat next to the window. I had watched the seasons change, saw the plants turn shades of green as they crawled up the solarium's twenty-foot-high windows. Finally I could touch the curling vines. I inhaled the dank, loamy fragrance and sat down on a perch made from branches.

I should have thought of an escape route, but I had been too focused on a photograph, the angle, the seconds I needed for exposure. I suddenly heard the sound of heavy steps. It might be only one person … a chance for sympathy? Could I squirm into the branches or run to the side door? Not enough time. A large man in green overalls walked in with the big clippers in his hand. Surprised, he stopped. My fears exploded; he could report me to the school, I would be in trouble again. The last time I had gotten into trouble had been a month before—I had left school at lunchtime and returned an hour late, after I had wandered into Central Park to watch the horses trot on the reservoir path. A horse had fallen, making me forget about school.

"You do something like that again and you could be put on probation," my teacher sternly told me, echoing my mother. "You're always in trouble, always in the wrong place. Why, Joanie? Why can't you be like the others?"

The gardener held my fate in his big rough hands. Perhaps it was my pleading expression that brought a slow smile to his face; maybe he knew I was supposed to be a "good girl" from the fancy school next door. Putting his finger to his lips, he motioned me to quietly follow him down the stairs. He pointed to a narrow door. I could hear the traffic sounds on Fifth Avenue.

Before pushing the door open for me, the gardener paused, giving me a kindly look. He spoke in a low voice.

"You know this is a place hidden to most people, only open to family and friends. I have a niece a little older than you who also wants to come here; maybe both of you will be invited some day."

"Thank you, sir. The gate was open. I had to come in," I stuttered.

As I turned to walk through the door to the street, the gardener touched my shoulder. "Don't worry; I won't tell your school."

My mother also liked hidden places. She once took me to The New York Doll Hospital, in a building on Lexington Avenue in the 60s.

We went there because of the accident. It happened one afternoon when she and I were strolling with my doll Bertha. On crossing Park Avenue, a taxi got too close and swerved, making me tip over the carriage. Bertha fell out, crashing onto the cement pavement. I gave out a cry as I knelt down to pick her up; her face was broken, her arm displaced. Mother helped me, told me it was going to be all right, that we'd think of something, as she brushed away the dirt on Bertha's dress.

"Come on, I know what we'll do. We'll take a cab down to the doll hospital, it's not far."

We arrived at the entrance and left the carriage downstairs for the climb up to the second floor, the pieces of Bertha in my arms. The banged-up door had a picture of a fancy doll in a big hoop skirt etched into its glass. A bell announced us. An old man came shuffling out through the beaded curtains, a dirty apron over his baggy pants. He didn't smile but nodded at us, giving a glance to Bertha, "*Ja, ja*, we can fix her," he said in a gruff German accent.

He didn't ask, but I told him about the accident anyway.

"*Ja*, those taxis. Her eye is broken," he said as he examined her. "You'll have to pick out some new eyeballs—up there, hanging from the ceiling. I'll get you a stepping stool." Mother started up the steps and gave a yell, not at the haphazardly falling eyeballs, but at the tiny animal darting past her hand.

"Oh, *ja,* no worry. This is old building. We have many furry friends. We all live here together. So now, little girl, find some new hair over there in the drawer, then we look for a new arm. You have another dress?"

He fiddled and pushed and pulled on Bertha.

"Okay, nice doll, old, good porcelain."

"She belonged to me, when I was a little girl—in the South," Mother told him, but received no reply.

"Come back in a week. Pay later. Bye-bye, very busy."

Mother pulled my arm toward the door, hiding giggles behind her hand.

New York offered easy access to spying adventures for young girls. My friends Tania, Shermane, and I wandered the streets and alleys and took the subway—all good places for people-watching and hearing foreign languages, especially Chinese and Spanish. We were intrigued by anything different from us.

At times we shouted to each other above the rumbling noise of the "el" train until it was torn down in 1955. On Friday afternoons we would walk slowly as we ogled the odd people we spied on our way to the grandeur of Broadway's Roxy Theatre. A man in a Viking suit wearing a helmet and antlers walked down Seventh Avenue like it was ordinary attire; a hoop-skirted and lipsticked woman stood on a busy corner loudly singing a Caribbean song while straining to control her three big dogs. Hardly anyone paid attention. We walked up behind her and pretended we were singing too. She thought we were making fun of her, which we were. But we also were in awe of people's daring; we wanted to be Vikings, or Caribbean singers, or something exotic.

Broadway was colorful and showy, compared to the staid greys, blacks, and browns of uptown. Park Avenue doormen tried to look intimidating in their dark winter, military-style long coats. And perhaps they were told not to smile, especially at children, because they needed to look as if they were guarding the building's deepest secrets. My friends and I took pride in knowing a few of the secrets; after all, we were spies. Lisa, who lived in a building at 60th and Park, had been told about a murder in a private ballroom. The dead woman had been taken down the back elevator and loaded into a delivery truck, bound for the East River. The word from the doorman was there would be no investigation. We also knew about the goats that lived in the big garden atop the penthouse of an apartment building on 73rd Street; no one knew how the goats got up there. But the secret we liked the best was about a couple having a fight at midnight. She threw his underwear out the window onto 74th Street. Lisa's father, Mr. Remnon, happened to be walking below. A gargoyle on the side of the building caught the underwear in flight. Mr. Remnon said the red boxers brightened up the building immensely. The image made us laugh.

Beginning in the second grade, Nanny and I, along with Shermane and her nanny, went to The Stork Club for Saturday lunch. Owned by Shermane's father, The Stork Club was a swanky nightspot on 53rd Street where movie stars, newspapermen looking for a story, and fancy society people gathered. The room was filled with the glamorous clinking of glasses, sophisticated chatter, and a haze of cigarette smoke. Famous people visited our table to say hi to the beloved daughter. Mr. Billingsley liked Shermane's friends, and always waited patiently for me to remove my stubborn right glove and shake his hand. He, Shermane, and I started The Schmo-Knucklehead Club and her father even had stationery made with the club's name embossed at the top. Mr. Billingsley's somewhat shady reputation as a bootlegger made no sense to me, but the stories added to his allure. Mrs. Billingsley didn't partake of the glamorous life we were allowed to glimpse. I only saw her a few times at their East 69th Street town house. Shermane said her mother spent most of her time in her private bedroom listening to Billy Graham and other radio evangelists.

But all that ended when I was twelve.

"You can't go to The Stork Club anymore," Mother said one afternoon.

"What do you mean? Shermane's my friend!" I cried.

"I know, and Mr. Billingsley has created such a lovely place, so beautiful and respectful—but it is café society."

"What's that?" I exclaimed.

Shermane's birthday at The Stork Club

"It means it's racy, too sophisticated and not right for a girl your age. It isn't proper."

"But we go to the 21 Club and Father told me that's sophisticated."

"That's different. Your father does business with 21. We feel comfortable there." Her decision was final.

But even at twelve, I knew that "café society" was somewhere I wanted to be.

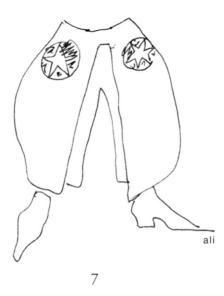

7

Eddie Doesn't Dance

I rang the elevator buzzer in the apartment vestibule. Eddie, my blind date for my first dance, was downstairs waiting for me.

Julio had called up on the building telephone to say that a young man had arrived.

"He's carrying a small white flower box," Julio whispered into the phone. "It must be a corsage." He chuckled.

Mother had arranged this date. Her friends had just returned to New York from a ten-year stay in England. Their son Eddie, like me age twelve, didn't know anyone in New York.

"Wouldn't it be nice if he would be your escort to the Get-Togethers Dance?" she asked.

"I don't know," I semi-whined, "he might be awful. What does he look like? Is he nice? Where will he go to school?" But since I had no other plan for a date, I said, "Okay. I suppose so."

"I'm sure he's nice. His parents are our friends and they wouldn't have an awful son," Mother insisted.

"Why not? You don't know, you've never even seen him," I argued.

"You'll have fun," she declared. She continued talking very rapidly about the new dress I would wear and reminded me that I had chosen it.

I wanted to go to the dance, an almost-adult event. Mother and I had gone to the tea at Mrs. Mortimer's to meet the committee who would or would not accept me as an invitee. Mother said I acted very grown up. I had wanted *her* to be the strength I could hide behind, but she wasn't. She hardly spoke.

I was excited to dress up, to wear my new fancy shoes with bows on the toes and be with my friends. I liked dancing school and I was good at dancing; everyone said so, even though I was taller than most of the boys.

As I waited by the elevator, Mother came out to say goodbye and to tell me I looked pretty in my green velvet dress, that my shoes looked just right.

"All the boys will want to dance with you. Those dances you practiced at dancing school ... you'll have fun. But, Joanie, I have something to tell you that I just learned."

As she leaned over to arrange the bows on the bottom of my skirt, I looked down at her newly combed wavy hair and inhaled her perfume.

"Eddie doesn't dance," she said quietly.

I stood there thinking I hadn't heard her right.

"What do you mean?" I stammered. "Of course he dances, if we're going to a dance." I pushed her away, feeling the tears start. "I've never been to a dance. He has to dance. What will we do?" I choked back a sob. "I'm not going."

She stood up.

"Of course you're going, and you'll have fun. Oh, Joanie, I'm sorry. It's a shame that Eddie doesn't dance," she pronounced the words slowly and looked away. "But wipe your eyes now, be brave, you're a big girl." I could hear the fake lightness in her tone.

"It's not just about dancing. You'll think of things to talk about. His school, his sports in England; ask him what he likes to do."

Why didn't she worry about me, my disappointment?

Eddie stood by the building's front door with the flower box in his hand. We shook hands and I took the corsage and held it. He didn't pin it on me. He looked nice, sort of handsome, especially with his longer-than-American-boys' hair. His dark suit was okay except his pants were too short. I knew that boys had trouble with pant length because their legs grow too fast. Anyway, that's what Mother said. I liked his striped black-and-white tie and the white carnation in his jacket's left buttonhole. He was taller than me, just the right height for a dance partner.

We arrived at The Plaza Hotel in a taxi that Eddie paid for with two crumpled dollar bills from his pocket. Although awkward in the cab, I felt grown up as I stepped out onto the green carpeted stairs that rose to the hotel's entrance, and I was proud to tell Eddie that The Persian Room to the left of the front door was where my parents had taken me to hear Judy Garland.

He just smiled.

I saw friends from school in the ballroom and I introduced Eddie. He told my friend Abby that he didn't dance. Abby said she was sorry and shot me a look of sympathy as her boyfriend Timmy pulled her over to his friends. I was jealous.

Eddie and I sat on the side in the line of cream-colored dressy chairs. The music started with a foxtrot. Mr. deRham, our dancing instructor, had told me I had rhythm, and Mr. deRham never said anything nice except to a few favorites—and I wasn't one of them.

We watched the dancing. Eddie didn't apologize or give me a reason for not dancing. I thought maybe he had broken his leg or foot at some time, and missed the classes, but I didn't ask. Or maybe he had told his mother he was going to dance classes and only confessed the lie on the night of our party. Or his mother knew and, just like my mother, didn't say anything until it was too late. It didn't occur to me then, but now I wonder—if it had been a girl who couldn't dance, would the boy have to escort her anyway?

I wanted to join the "line dance" as a solo, but that might not be correct. I had been taught at dancing school to fold my hands in my lap, to look demure and interested in the boy, so I tried that. I struggled to think of conversation, as Mother had told me to do.

"Is it really cold in England?"

"Yes," he answered, "and it rains a lot." He liked talking about cricket, a game I didn't understand but he described. I was glad his explanation took a long time. He told me how miserable he was, being away from his school friends.

"Why did my parents have to come back to New York?" he asked. I couldn't answer, and by then, I didn't care.

My lavender corsage, now sitting carelessly on my lap, had wilted. No one asked me to dance. They all had partners. In today's atmosphere, I wouldn't have to wait. I could ask a boy to dance. But at that time it would have been considered aggressive; a girl must wait for the boy.

I prayed Eddie and I could leave soon.

And Mother was wrong. We didn't have any fun, it was misery. I held back the tears until I arrived home. She apologized again and said she hadn't known Eddie couldn't dance. I didn't believe her. It was a quiet betrayal, the subtle hint that as the girl, my feelings didn't count, not really. Eddie didn't dance. Boys are not your playmates anymore, not like they were when you were six, or even eleven.

"You want them to like you, Joanie, don't you?"

"Yes," I answered. I wanted boys to like me.

A few weeks later my Aunt Beezie, who lived a few blocks down the street from us, confirmed what Mother had already told me when I complained about Eddie's conversation.

"Boys aren't very good at questions." Beezie said. "In fact, men hardly ask questions, at least not to women, except for my sweet husband, but he *is* my third husband." She and Mother laughed.

Mother added, "It's not so much about conversation, Joanie. That doesn't mean they don't want you to have a good time; it's just the way they are. They like to talk about sports—boy things." She told me that girls were more mature than boys, and maybe Eddie was just shy. Aunt Beezie put her hand under my chin and gave me a kiss. She and Mother left the room chatting and giggling, and I heard Beezie say, "Twelve years old, Lordy, what a difficult age."

And it was. Life was much easier when I was just Cactus Pete.

My father had honored my cowboy persona of Cactus Pete by giving me a set of off-white leather holsters covered in glittery rhinestones that held my almost-real-looking Colt 45s. He said the gun belt was custom made. On nights when there were small gatherings at home—especially for Southerners—Father would call out, "Cactus, go on and get your holsters, friends really want to see you twirl those guns."

Always ready for those moments, I ran to my room and quickly put on my outfit: a red-checked shirt with a bolo tie, my special red cowboy hat and, of course, the guns. Nervous to begin my performance, but also confident that I could twirl both guns at the same time—backwards first, then forwards, spinning them into the holsters—I stood tall and waited until the chatter quieted down to make my entrance. Aunt Billie, at the piano, would start to sing a few bars of *Happy Trails*. My routine was a success and the audience gave me a whistling applause. Cactus was a star.

Father called me Cactus, or just plain Pete, until he died. I had taken the name for granted until one day, well into my twenties, I asked him the name's source.

He teased me.

"There was a cowboy character named Cactus Pete. Funny lookin' thing, and wild. In the rodeo he would swing onto the horses, fall on the ground, get up and dust himself off, then do it again. As a little girl, you were always jumping on the back of the big old upholstered chair in the living room, pretending it was your horse. One day, you missed, kind of fell on the floor, got yourself up and backed up ten steps to run and jump on the chair again. I laughed so hard. From then on, for me, you were my little cherished Cactus Pete."

Soon after the danceless dance with Eddie, I put away Cactus' holsters. My perfect cowboy hat and the photograph of me at the age of nine on the twenty-five-cent bucking bronco ride—hat waving in a high salute—were relegated to the closet. The twelve-year-old Joanie was starting to understand what her place was supposed to be.

But I didn't want to know my place. The Magnolia Code and all the other codes were good for some people, lots of people maybe, but they weren't good for me. I wanted to know what was out in the world besides those rules. Aunt Billie had directed me—her drawl became ever more pronounced when making a point—"Joanie, you have got to look around you, see what you like, where you want to go. There are tough choices, and sometimes tough consequences, but you have to make them. Simple as that."

It wasn't easy to find examples of people who had turned away from the rules. In my adolescent years an older distant cousin, Frances Ann, a Southerner who had been the flower girl in my parents' wedding, became a role model. She rejected her textile family for their racist views and harsh treatment of workers in their North Carolina factory. She told me she walked into a board meeting and threw down her shares of the company's stock. She later married a famous author who was classified as a Communist and their eventual much-publicized divorce produced a scandal in my parent's circle. I loved her feistiness, her dares. And we became great friends in my late thirties.

My parents rarely talked about their views on politics or cultural ideas, although Mother was proud she had voted for Franklin Roosevelt, a vote that irked Father.

I'm sorry that I mostly remember them fighting. Perhaps, after a while, to them and to us, fighting had the sound of conversation. Only occasionally did I catch a glimpse of their intimate connection. It happened one night at an evening awards ceremony party at The Plaza Hotel. Father was one of the men being honored by the Boy Scouts. Alicia was home sick. I sat at the children's "nowhere" table off the ballroom. Restless, I sneaked away to look at the grownups dancing. I saw Father walk to the table where Mother was sitting. They looked at each other; his face had a kind look, not his usual I-am-about-to-make-fun expression. He held out his hand and she took it. The band was playing *From This Moment On*. I had heard him sing that song to her once when she was sad, when her good friend was dying.

Mother stood up at the table to meet him. He led her out to the dance floor and put his arm around her waist, tight like he did when he danced with us. They put their cheeks together. Father was a good leader. After he twirled her, she easily came back into step with him, all around the dance floor, and every time they parted, their eyes would find each other's smiling gaze.

I told Alicia the dancing story after overhearing one of their bad fights, when Alicia had started to cry. We hid in my bedroom.

She asked, "Why do they always fight? When they start yelling at each other, everything goes upside down. Why do they do that?"

"Maybe they just don't like each other," I said.

She blurted out that Father was fun, but Mother was not. I don't quite know why I came to Mother's rescue, but I said she could be fun, that we had fun when we were out on the street together.

"Maybe they don't know what to say to each other."

"Maybe not," Alicia said. "That's funny, isn't it?"

"Why's that funny?"

"I don't know. Seems they should know what to say to each other." Alicia played with her embroidered nightgown, the one with the yellow sunflowers. She looked unhappy. We wished we shared a room. Then we could whisper all night and not be scared.

Although Alicia was a year and a half older, we were raised like twins, our eyes open to protecting each other from our parents, sometimes the world. We didn't look alike, or act alike. She was shy. I—or at least my Cactus identity— was out there running down the street, talking to everyone. Alicia was skinny and tall, sometimes a bit frightened. But when her friend Sallie ran over her finger at Rockefeller Center skating rink, Alicia's big tears didn't last long. Feeling sorry for herself was not Alicia's way.

When I think of Alicia's abusive first marriage, I hear Billie's voice: "The world won't keep you safe, Joanie." Alicia had picked an unkind man to marry, a man who she thought would protect her, not abuse her, one she thought was a safe choice. Eleven years later, with three small children in tow and the courage given to her by a fine, caring man, she left the abuser and married the kind man.

But that night after our parents' fight, I wanted us both to feel better, so I told her almost with a plea, "I know it was just a moment, but I saw our parents, Alicia, I saw them dancing. They liked each other ... for a while, anyway."

"Wish I'd seen them," Alicia answered with a sniffle.

Years later, my boyfriend Dick and I were at Broadway's Roseland Ballroom. Our argument was getting loud. But the band started and we began to dance. Two bodies pressed up against each other. Nowhere to go except somewhere—for a moment—together.

8

Where you ever gonna belong, chile?

My eccentric and wild Uncle Itch loved to tease me on his journeys from the South to New York.

"You're just a little damn Yankee girl. Where you ever gonna belong, chile?" He laughed as he swung me up in the air, and even though I giggled, I was perplexed about what he meant; I just knew it wasn't good. I stored the question somewhere in my head.

I'd often heard it said the Deep South is not a place, it's an attitude. The promise of belonging to the Southern way had many appealing hooks. I knew some of the great traits of the South. The Southerner can tell a story, and the story always has a touch of magic. The storyteller invites you to sit down in a rocker on the porch, puts a cool drink in your hand, and offers the joy, sorrow, and yearning of a tale well told, complete with the particular rhythm and jazz of the South. Life seen through the Southern lens mixes romance, brutality, humor and compassion.

To react properly to a tale, you're expected to cry, belly-ache laugh, slap your thigh—and sometimes utter a plaintive "Yes'm" to the story's final words: "She killed that no-good husband, bless her heart. Why, he's nothin' but a damn fallin-down drunk."

Public persona is of utmost importance in the South. You better be ready to greet someone who might stop by, or, as Mother would say, "Joanie, always dress, no tellin' who you'll see at the dime store or even on the subway." I knew it was true that if you did see that someone, you were likely to feel a reciprocating ease and care in manner. I once asked Mother if the concept of "politely smudging the truth" meant that everything in the South was covered over in some sort of dewy magnolia scent. She didn't appreciate the query and told me to stop questioning everything.

"Accept life, Joanie. It is just as easy to follow the rules."

The Southern step has a lightness, a grace. And surely Mother's soft North Carolina accent was the prettiest I'd ever heard. A Southerner exudes hospitality and friendliness— although there is another opinion regarding this hospitality. A cousin who moved North said that behind the Southern graciousness lies hidden the violent undertones of the legacy of slavery. Aunt Billie would have added, "Don't fret about all this—history, our lifestyle; it's just moonlight and magnolias."

Uncle Itch was my father's youngest brother. His real name was Archie. I never questioned his nickname—everyone in the South seemed to have one. Uncle Itch was a medical doctor in the time when doctors still made house calls, and he was—unlike most doctors—willing, and even eager, to cross the invisible line into the black part of Jacksonville. To Alicia and me, he was a little scary, a big man with a slightly smashed-in face who drank too much but was funny and lovable.

Everything about Uncle Itch was Southern: the storytelling, the drinking, the laughing, his larger-than-life presence.

Although we hardly ever went south to see Uncle Itch or other members of my father's family, but we often visited Mother's brother, Uncle Jack, and his wife, Aunt Luna, in Corwith.

Whenever we were in Corwith, I wondered what it would be like to grow up in the South. People my age there were different from my New York friends— at times so proper, so unbelievably polite. Alicia and I laughed at how they ended every sentence with "Ma'am" or "Sir."

"They sure do 'Ma'am' a lot," Alicia said.

But they also had a sultry, slightly improper side. On a visit when I was fourteen, Aunt Luna said Alicia and I could go off with two nice boys to the drive-in. It was a hot July night and we went to see the steamy 1958 film, *The Long Hot Summer*. It was that movie, a small jug of mint juleps, and the kisses I exchanged with Knox in the back seat of his car that made the experience memorable. I missed the point of the movie, but the film exactly represented the languid spirit of the South where everything seemed to move slow there.

Aunt Luna also made sure we went to a dance or two. Southern boys danced differently from northern ones. Maybe the heat slowed the dancing, but our hot hands held onto each other tightly and the sweet-nothing whispering was dreamy, calculated to make you think you were "the one." All of that Southernness comprised a sensuality that was new to me.

"They're taught to behave that way; I think it's the humidity," Aunt Billie laughed. "Anyway, they get to you. Your father has that charm. You just can't resist it."

I liked the taste of mint juleps. On summer nights in the country, Father would tell Alicia and me, "Go cut me some mint; get the pretty ones, no brown tips. Now, take that hammer, Joanie, and crush those ice cubes." He would laugh as I put my strength into hitting the ice bag on the floor. Father then added the sugar, mint, and bourbon, slowly pouring the liquid over the slivers of ice into a silver goblet used just for mint juleps. I must have taken too many sips when Father wasn't looking, as I now hate the scent and taste of bourbon. But I have kept those goblets.

Aunt Luna and Uncle Jack had stayed on in Corwith. They had no desire to leave the South. Their home—Mother and Uncle Jack's growing-up house—became a meaningful center of town for times of fun, cocktails and civic concern. Aunt Luna was full of life. She moved around her everything-must-be-painted-puce kitchen with ease, baking and frying, never bothering to take off her big jeweled rings—"dinner rings," she called them, though she wore them all the time, so they weren't just for dinnertime. A huge pin of butterflies with sapphires and rubies peaked over the top of her apron. I told her I loved that pin; she said she'd leave it to me when that fine day came when the Lord might call her to

Mother's family home

heaven. Aunt Luna was never underdressed. Around the house she wore a thin flowered cotton skirt and matching top, cool for the Carolina heat, but no matter what the temperature, she always had on stockings and low-heeled, slightly fancy shoes. That was the Southern woman's look, "always ready for hospitality," Mother said.

Alicia and I would sit on the porch swing on either side of Aunt Luna, swaying back and forth, hoping to catch a breeze to offset that stifling humidity. Between Aunt Luna's big jangly bracelets on her left arm and the stabbing rings on her right hand, her squeezes—made whenever she wanted to punctuate a thought—made us yell, "Ow, Aunt Luna, ow, ow, that hurts!"

"Lawsy, what's the matter with you two pretty little girls, it's just a sweet ol' love squeeze."

Where you ever gonna belong, chile?

The porch, fifteen feet from the sidewalk, was long and wide enough to have two seating areas and a table in the middle, always with beautiful cut-glass bowls on it—one for pecans and another for cheese straws. People walking in front of the house would call out, "Hey there, Miss Luna, what you doing on this hot day? Those your two favorite nieces?"

"Yes'm, they surely are, and we are just havin' the best of times, right now enjoying some sweet ice tea," Aunt Luna would call back. "Y'all come onto the porch and join us, if you like. If you don't want ice tea, the other decanter is full of sherry." The scent from the mint hanging over the edges of our silver tea goblets and the sweet fragrance of the camellias, cut and displayed on an elegant blue-and-white plate, gave the setting an atmosphere of Southern graciousness. Everything at Aunt Luna's evinced comfort and beauty.

Aunt Luna's nonstop discourse was interrupted and exaggerated by rolling laughs. I especially remember a story she told me during one visit, while she was making aspic for lunch.

"I just came from the jail and I told that judge, I said, 'Judge, my cook Cora should have shot that man, she was absolutely right. Why, I encouraged her, Judge, him mean as a snake like that to her. Sometimes you just got to, who cares the consequences. Shoot him again, I say. And, anyway, he's not even dead.' "

"You really told that to the judge? What did he say?" I asked, wide-eyed.

"Good grief, he just said something moronic about laws and that it's up to the police. So I said to him, 'So when are the police on the side of my wonderful Cora? Just tell me that, Judge, go on, tell me!'

"But Joanie, right about then my anger was too hot, boiling up in me. I thought I'd better leave. I mean, what are those people thinking? Well, they're not thinking, just their own stupid thoughts is all. That judge, oh, he's probably head of the KKK."

With that Aunt Luna quietly edged across the room to take a nip from the glass of bourbon she had hidden behind the puce radio. She thought I wasn't looking and I pretended I wasn't.

"But Aunt Luna, I know you say damn the outcome, but what will happen to Cora?"

"Oh Lord, I don't know. I do want to scream sometimes. Just stand up and scream. It hurts my heart for Cora."

"Sometimes, Aunt Luna, I want to scream, too. Last week I was at a school concert and I wanted to yell right in the middle of it—just to see people's reactions, or to see if I'd faint. I wanted to scream—and then walk out."

Aunt Luna looked at me and then "fell out" laughing, as she would say.

"Oooh, I'd love to see your mother's face, oooh, she'd have a fit, she would just have herself a fit to see you scream, Sis being so proper and ladylike." She paused and gave me a thoughtful look. "But she probably wants to scream herself ... I think about her, Joanie, yes, I do."

"You do, what do you think about her?"

"Oh, she's never been very happy, and I'm sorry for that. She cares too much what other people think, all those rules. She's stuck and she can't scream."

"I'm not very good at rules. I get in trouble a lot."

"Well, you have to follow some rules, that's for sure. But sometimes you got to choose, best thing is to stand up for yourself, and that can be plum hard, just like Cora shooting that ornery husband and, well, just like this cooking lesson here. There you are writing things down like it's an actual recipe ... but there just isn't any recipe. I said, 'throw in a world of salt, give the pan a big shake, butter, butter—Lord, put in a load of butter—and that's it.' Now, you can't really write that down, can you Joanie? You have to get the feel for cooking, like choosing—you have to choose what feels good."

I listened and laughed, and thought about what she called feel-good choices. I figured I would learn to make the cake another time. Although they had little in common, Aunt Luna—like Aunt Billie—gave me something Mother just didn't have to offer: encouragement to make my own choices, a sense that I had value, that I could be my own person.

"Oh, Lord, best get this fried chicken on the stove," she said suddenly. "I make the best fried chicken. You knows that, everybody knows that," she chuckled to herself. "Go on, explain more about what you think of rules, I can do two things at once. But I want to tell you that you just gotta know what lives down deep inside you—and then take a chance."

Where you ever gonna belong, chile?

9

Ain't nothin' happen here, lady

After college, my curiosity about my upbringing and my confusion of choices and paths grew. Could I understand my parents' Southern values? I got the chance to explore my questions further with my good friend Cynthia, who was from Alabama.

It all started when Cynthia and I argued about whose aunt made the best mayonnaise.

"Andrew's visiting me from England next week. Let's just go, let's show him the South," she proposed. She dubbed the trip the Homemade Mayonnaise Cook-off Journey. Andrew, the foreigner, would be the judge.

On a hot May afternoon in 1965, the three of us drove our rental car into a gas station in Selma, Alabama. The big-paunched, very white gas attendant looked over at me while he was pumping gas.

"You fixin' to do something to this car? Tires look mighty down. Needs help, just like that old Chevy over there," he said, chuckling and nodding toward a long-dead truck with a big vine sticking out the front window. "Same as me," he yawned, "plum wore out."

"Gas will do it right now, thanks," I said. "We're heading toward Georgia; just came across the bridge there." I pointed toward the Selma bridge. "Pretty important spot right there, isn't it? King and the march," I said with assurance.

The attendant wiped his hands slowly on a dirty cloth and gave me a sideways sneer.

"Ain't nothin' happen on that bridge, ain't nothin' happen here, lady. You hear me? Now why don' you jes pay for the gas and git on down the road, don't make me more tired."

I got back into the car.

"Jesus, that man is scary, let's get out of here," spat out Andrew.

"Dirty bigot, what does he know?" Cynthia added.

But what did we really know of the march across the Selma bridge? We knew the names, we knew who the heroes were: Martin Luther King, Jr., Rosa Parks, the four young girls who died in a church fire in Birmingham, the white people and celebrities who joined the march. We had pictures in our memories, TV images of attacking dogs, hatred on the faces of white boys and girls jeering at black students entering the newly integrated University of Alabama.

Were we naïve? Were we insensitive to the angry man, dismissing him as just a racist, not giving a care for his fear that the black man was gaining power over him, might take his job, might even marry his daughter? We were three privileged young white people with not-well-thought-out questions about civil rights. What was the reality of black versus white life in the South?

By the time we reached Highway 90 and took a right to Monticello, Georgia, my grandmother's birthplace, and had stopped to talk to people at fruit stands, cafés, and a hardware store, our gap of understanding was slowly—very slowly—beginning to diminish.

The guidebook said Monticello was "Deep South cotton plantation country," a small town of tree-lined streets, antebellum homes, even an opera house. I knew nothing was left of Grandmother's family plantation; it had been burned down in the Civil War.

I hardly knew her. Grandmother died when I was seven, but I remember her petite yet formidable presence. She would visit us in the summer and we would write poetry and prose together, or at least she kindly included me as one of the "authors." Her topics were history and family, and everything she wrote bore a religious undertone. One of her short stories was about Mammy, her children's nurse, who had been born a slave. She loved Mammy in that Southern way, with compassion and care, but with an assured belief that Mammy's plight in life was

God's will. To Grandmother, Mammy was childlike and lived only to serve and honor the family.

In "My Memories of Mammy," Grandmother wrote that on Mammy's hundredth birthday, she had asked her, "Mammy, what do you want the Lord to give you when you go up to heaven?"

Mammy replied to Grandmother, without hesitation, "I wants a pretty garden full of li'l chillun and I hopes my Jesus will let me be de Mammy ob dem all—and dats all I wants."

We stopped outside Monticello by the banks of the unspoiled Suwannee River. The three of us lay in the grass, dreaming in that hot, half-asleep time of afternoon. The words of the gas attendant, "Ain't nothin happen here, lady," were lost for the moment. I imagined my grandmother on her family's veranda, looking out over the plantation's lush green toward the beckoning cool stream on a summer's day—a bucolic life, really. For her, the day on the Selma bridge was in the far-off future. I thought of family moments and Uncle Itch's teasing words, "Where you ever gonna belong, chile?"

The South I was experiencing was seductive; part of its allure was the illusion of familiarity and safety. But I knew it was a trap that I had to resist.

One of the books I had re-read for our Southern journey was the story of Br'er Rabbit from *Tales of Uncle Remus* (written by Joel Chandler Harris, a white man). Years before—I was probably seven—my family visited our cousin's plantation in South Carolina. I particularly remember the Spanish moss hanging from every tree shadowing the endless porch. Alicia and I wanted to run into the fields, but cousin Jim Davis said the snakes had come out in full force that year.

"Instead, y'all go on with Old Joe here back to the barn; he's gonna read you some stories 'bout Br'er Rabbit. We call Joe 'Uncle Remus' cuz of his beautiful white head o' hair and beard."

I looked at Joe's old, lined, dark brown face, saw him nod and heard a chuckle.

"Yes'm, y'all can call me Uncle Remus."

Alicia and I sat with him in the barn and listened intently to the stories, mesmerized by his speech, not caring that we could hardly understand a word.

In the stories, Br'er Rabbit was portrayed as a trickster fooling his fellow animals, but I have recently learned that the tales were actually created in order to teach slaves how to overcome their "marsters," how with their cleverness and inner resources they could outwit the authorities. White people thought the anecdotes were sweet tales for children, not realizing they were lessons in survival.

What would Br'er Rabbit's creativity say to the man who boasted, "Ain't nothin happen here, lady?" The three of us pondered the question, but we weren't clever—or scared enough, as a black person might have been—to know the answer.

Throughout the trip Andrew fiddled with the radio, obsessed with finding the local gospel stations.

"Bessie Smith, can't we find her?" Andrew mumbled.

"Have you ever heard Nina Simone sing *Strange Fruit*?" Cynthia asked. "It's a song white Southerners don't want to know about. 'Black bodies swinging in the southern breeze/Strange fruit hangin' from the poplar trees,' " Cynthia sang.

With this new information, we silently drove on in the lush beauty of Georgia and crossed the border into the middle part of South Carolina—agricultural country—then into the eastern part of the state, where the scent of the sea, not ten miles away, was heady. We were north of Charleston about an hour, headed for the home of Cynthia's Aunt Emma, one of the mayonnaise makers. Her house was planted on the banks of the tidal river, the Cooper. Cynthia told us that it was the only house left standing on the family's large rice plantation.

"She's lived there forever, married a handsome farmer, a real character named Rabbit."

"Another Rabbit?" asked Andrew.

"This Rabbit's a charmer with a lot of luck, some say. Wait 'til you see their plantation."

The cook, Yvette, greeted us and said that Aunt Emma was "lyin' low" and sick in bed with the shades drawn.

"But Mr. Rabbit, he's takin' care of y'all, nothin' he loves more than that."

Rabbit showed us around the plantation, the rice fields, the former slave quarters and the mill. He told stories about the Southern bravery and the Civil War battles on their land.

"And Yvette, she prepares a great dinner every few months for our group. We call ourselves The Boys of Dixie."

"What do you mean?" I asked.

"The dinner? It's for the memory of those who fought valiantly in the War Between the States. We sit around, tell stories, drink a bit."

"And Yvette caters the dinner? A black woman cooking for all of you while you sing *Dixie*?" I blurted.

Our mouths were open with the incredulousness of his insensitivity.

"How's that?" Rabbit asked with a questioning stare. "She doesn't mind, we're good to sweet Yvette, we love her," he said, his voice rising with irritation.

On our return to the house, we immediately went to Yvette and asked about her catering for The Boys of Dixie.

"How could you do that for those entitled little 'boys?'" I asked her.

"I did, I made some good money. But I do have a story for you, ya'll gonna like this," Yvette answered. "For about five years I catered that party, cooked fried chicken, barbecue, all the fixin's, and those men, they just loved it all. I heard the stories they were saying 'bout us—colored folk this, colored folk that, and having themselves a laugh. At first I didn't really care cuz I charged them a heap of money, maybe a little more than usual, them bein' who they were. So all was fine until one day I walked into Mr. Rabbit's office room. A new toy sat on the floor at the door. And y'all know what that was? It was one of those little nigger boys, 'bout a foot tall, holding the door. That was it. I said to Mr. Rabbit, 'What do y'all think y'all doing with that doorstop? You just take that and throw it somewhere.' I was deep-down mad. Mr. Rabbit, well he got himself into an angry place, too, and said that he didn't mean anything by it and he would put it somewhere, but not that night, he said, 'Because the boys are coming for dinner and they gave it to me.'

"So, I thought and thought," Yvette went on. "I made them boys a stew, a very good okra stew, but I added—not just a little, but a cupful of a special herb. You know the one, the herb that treats constipation—called senna. After dinner when I saw them all runnin' for the bathroom, I had myself the biggest laugh. And that was that. That little black boy went into the trash and nothin' more was said."

We were bent over laughing.

"Oh, that's so good, Yvette," I said. "Guess they were stupid enough to not understand the meaning of, 'Never say anything bad to the chef.' "

Yvette rubbed her neck and we were quiet, awaiting her response.

"You know, there's that little spot in all of us where we just don't recognize our own weakness." She paused.

"Oh, I almost forgot, your Aunt Emma made you some mayonnaise yesterday before she took to her bed."

I glanced over at Cynthia and Andrew. The mayonnaise contest was on, despite Aunt Emma's "infirmity."

"Oh, Yvette, one more thing. Tomorrow's Sunday, do you think we could go to the black church in town?" I asked. "We'd love to hear the music."

"Hmmm, that might be real hard right now with all the trouble. I'm not too sure you'd be welcome." She hesitated. "But you could park outside. The music's plenty loud comin' through the open windows. Y'all could do that—but I wouldn't mention it to Mr. Rabbit."

Aunt Emma still felt ill the next morning, but we called to her through the bedroom door that we were walking to church a few blocks away. She thought we meant her Presbyterian Church.

"Oh well, that's probably a good thing, but I warn you, that minister could bore the curl right out of your hair."

"Aunt Emma, we just tasted your delicious mayonnaise," Cynthia called, winking at us.

"I am delighted. When you return, I'll be up and we'll make a kitchen-sink tomato sandwich. Do you know what that is?"

"Can't imagine," Andrew said.

"So, you see, you put so much mayonnaise on the tomato sandwich, you have to lean over the sink to let the mayonnaise run down your arm." We could hear Aunt Emma give herself a big laugh.

Sitting in a discreet place under the trees, we watched as churchgoers in elaborate hats, fancy dresses, and striped business suits emerged from cars and swayed a bit to the music leading them inside the church.

We heard the minister start.

"Today we're going to celebrate the rivers, particularly our beautiful Cooper Tidal River here in Medford. We give thanks to this water of life that gives energy to our crops and to the beauty of the land. And with equal importance, we recognize the river as a symbol of freedom, as the good Bible tells us. Here we go, the choir will begin our thanks this morning with Sam Cooke's new song of courageous protest, *A Change is Gonna Come.*"

The choir sang and the band played; the congregation joined in. The lines of the chorus rang out:

> *I was born by the river in a little tent*
> *Oh, and just like the river I've been runnin' ever since*
> *It's been a long, a long time comin'*
> *But I know a change gon' come, oh yes it will.*

Heading north from Aunt Emma's for a visit to Cynthia's cousin Robin gave us more moments of Southern wonder—good and bad—and provided more tastes of the relatives' homemade mayonnaise. No one really won the contest.

"It's a draw," Andrew said politely.

One day at noon we experienced a disturbing moment. Parked by a dusty roadside café in the middle of nowhere, Andrew went in to find seats. A room on the left was filled with five tables of white people eating just what we wanted—grits and sausage. The man behind the counter looked at Andrew, heard his English accent and said, with that same sneer we'd heard at the Selma bridge gas station, "Yeah, we're open but we don't serve lunch."

Andrew started his retort with, "I don't understand, I see all those people—" but he quickly knew to walk out, feeling the man's piercing eyes on the back of his beige linen jacket.

Hurrying to the car, Andrew reported, "Plenty of room, they don't serve lunch, scary, let's go."

"And that's just the way it is down here in the genteel South," said Cynthia.

10

The Curved Settee

After our eye-opening trip to the South, I returned to New York, where it seemed like most of my friends were racing for the altar. "Ring by spring or your money back" had been the faux motto of our college. Instead of this path, a school roommate and I started our anticipated ascent into other cultures, beginning as students in Florence. We longed to speak Italian fluently and to lose ourselves in some sort of idyllic foreign life.

Mainly art history students, we also took Italian history courses and read Dante with an adored tutor, Signorina Panella, who sat across from us at a little table as we read and she corrected.

By spring we had left the "proper" students-sent-abroad housing at the Marchesa Patrizi's and, with one other American student, rented a hillside apartment with a tiny terrace overlooking the olive orchards in Fiesole, outside Florence. It was an idyllic time. We had Italian boyfriends who expected nothing but some sweet kisses. An elderly and charming Englishman bought us grappa at the bus drivers' bars in Florence, wrote poetry describing us as "the oyster's pearls," and occasionally sneaked us into formal British Consulate parties. Our cheap Victrola, bought in the Florence flea market, played *Ne Me Quitte Pas*— the height of romantic songs, sung by my idol, Nina Simone—over and over. I didn't mind that the ashes falling from my cigarette created little skips on the 33rpm disc.

We celebrated Easter in an ancient building said to have been created by Michelangelo and was now a chic hotel. I remember the magnificently curved settee that anchored the middle of the sixteenth-century Italian living room. Springtime fragrances wafted their way up from the village of Fiesole. While Katharine, one of our threesome, wandered the hotel's gardens, my friend Beth and I slumped down on the settee to a half-nap after the splurge of a Sunday lunch and some sort of delicious white wine that kept appearing in our glasses.

The old-fashioned settee had a high, carved center separating its two seating areas, thus making Beth and me invisible to the couple who sat down on the opposite side, and immediately began to whisper of long-lost love. The amorous words, spoken in a slow enough Italian for us to understand, painted a picture. They hadn't seen each other in forty years. As much as they had tried to forget and live their lives with their spouses, their love for one another had never diminished. Now here they were, meeting by surprise as each spent the holiday with family.

"Life could have been otherwise," we heard him mourn. "And you still wear the same perfume."

"And you still have beautiful hands," she said.

It was a moment when young women usually fall into nervous giggles, but we didn't. The poignancy of their words stopped us.

"Perhaps we still have a chance," he suggested with hope. There was silence. I wondered if she had reached for his hands. We waited silently, transfixed. It would be terrible if they now knew of our existence.

They did not remain on the settee for long. We could hear a sense of urgency in their voices; they knew their spouses would soon be looking for them. We heard an appointed time to meet later, somewhere down the road.

"Yes, I remember the little park, up the hill, off to the left," she said. A stillness pervaded the room. Had they reached over for a hurried kiss?

I can see the room. I can smell the blossoms and delectable food mixed with the aroma of rich after-lunch espressos. I cannot see them, as I couldn't then, but I imagine them: she with greying wavy hair pulled back in a soft bun, wearing a graceful skirt, a striped silk blouse, an old-fashioned brooch at the collar; he in a checked cashmere jacket and dark brown, well-fitting pants, his hair thinning. Both have on Italian shoes of buttery leather. Their appearance matches the elegance of the hotel.

I can still hear the gently spoken words of romance—a memory perhaps accentuated by a little too much wine that day—but we also heard the sorrow of unlived lives.

Beth and I didn't get up from the settee until well after the couple had left the room. We sat with our thoughts, neither of us sure what to say. Back in our apartment in Fiesole, I looked down from our narrow balcony and caught the scent of the ancient olive trees, wondering what the world would offer the couple. Were the obstacles they faced too difficult? At my age, the future looked confusing but positive, but the overheard conversation rang with the despair of wrong choices in the past.

The world of my parents—the betrayals, the façades, the bowing to safety and conventional codes—had been portrayed to me, slowly but surely, as the real world.

"This is the way it is, Joanie," Mother said, in her trying-to-be-light tone. "We don't speak out loud about our problems. Oh, that dark dramatic side you see in movies, that's just for the movies. You'd better figure out your own troubles."

Part of me believed her. But I knew of a letter she had recently received from a woman she didn't know. Mother told Alicia about the note.

"Dear Mrs. Baker, I need to relieve myself of my guilt. I am writing to tell you that I will no longer be seeing your husband. I'm sorry for any pain I have caused."

"Why would Mother show this to you?" I implored Alicia.

"Maybe only because I was there that day. And who else could she tell?" Women didn't confide in each other about such things, not then. Mother couldn't even ask for the minister's help; that would be considered a betrayal, as Father was a respected deacon in the church.

Sometimes women like Mother went mad. They couldn't find the courage to confront their husbands, and the fear of loneliness and lack of support must have been overwhelming. They were trapped, struggling alone. Society found it easy to blame or mock women for their hurt, more so if they exhibited "hysteria"—as Mother once did when she chased Father down Park Avenue, screaming at him after overhearing a phone call to another woman. As he reached his parked car and drove off, Mother stood on the street, suddenly silent, alone with her rage.

How could Father be so callous? Didn't he care about Mother, or was his need to justify his actions made simpler by blaming her? With us he was warm and loving; I remember him waiting for me at the bottom of Margaret's Falls as I, a little girl of six, sat in the freezing water, searching for the courage to push off and slide down the tiny waterfall.

"Come on Joanie," he had said, gesturing to me. "I'll catch you. Don't worry, I'm right here."

I trusted him completely.

11

Louise and Terence

Toward the end of my year of studies in Florence, I had a fairly strong urge to join the Peace Corps, the organization founded during the Kennedy administration that provides assistance to various countries. Learning about other cultures and languages—that experience would be everything I liked and would fit me so well, I thought. But I didn't join, and I look back on that decision with regret. I can't remember the moment of decision, or even if there was an exact moment, but I do know my lack of self-worth rose up as a resulting self-criticism. Did I reject my idea from fear of commitment, or fear that I would be stuck somewhere for two years? Could I not make up my mind which path to follow—risk versus safety? What happened? Who was I? I was supposed to know by then, wasn't I?

Today I appreciate the humbling process of falling into self-doubt or self-sabotage. I now realize that personal evolution—if indeed we do evolve—does not follow a straight line.

Instead of the Peace Corps, I went to London and worked at odd jobs, and as a foreigner, was always paid under the table. Not overly interested in the English people or lifestyle, I felt restless and only truly enjoyed a two-month work stint at a financial firm, where I was thrown in with ten Cockneys sitting around a table calculating numbers. The first day we stared at each other, not understanding a word of each other's speech. After a week of miscommunication, we crossed a language barrier of sorts. Then I couldn't wait to be with these very funny people who told stories in a hilarious and self-effacing way and with a poetic rhythm. With our firm's minimal lunch vouchers, we went to their Cockney restaurants and then after work to their Cockney pubs, where I was meant to eat a favored eel-and-something dish—which, thankfully, I only had to endure once.

My mid-twenties was a fallow period, an on-the-fence, uninspired time of tending to my wandering soul. A week before I left London, Mother had said to buy something English—preferably china—for my future married life. I fell into the trappings of the Magnolia Code and bought twelve demitasse cups—which still stare at me from my kitchen's top shelf.

I returned to New York to a job on Wall Street, taken at Father's suggestion, where my work was to diagram the performance of each client's portfolio. The graphs were supposed to be simple, black-and-white renditions of progress or lack thereof, but instead I bought every design of colored and crisscrossed tape in the art store and had a joyous time creating what I believed were beautiful—but ultimately unappreciated—illustrations.

I knew I wasn't going to remain on Wall Street.

"Now the fun is over, you should do something worthwhile," Mother said. I had just turned twenty-four—I remember because it was my birthday—when Mother advised, "Joanie, you should just get married; you can always divorce."

I was stunned.

"What? Are you saying just marry someone, for the look of it? Then everything would be okay?"

"Well, maybe it won't work, but you could try. Sometimes you just quietly learn to love."

We were standing in the sunlit kitchen of my fourth-floor walk-up apartment. I didn't like her to visit; she felt free to criticize. She stood looking out the window as she offered her ill advice. I could see the side of her forlorn face—what was she really feeling?

Whenever the subject of marriage approached, I felt torn between my fear of marriage claustrophobia and its appeal—contained in a bowl of companionship, security, and a testimony to correctness. "This is the next step in life; my husband and I, we belong to each other," were phrases of proof I believed friends and my two older sisters uttered to themselves. Many acquaintances were marrying, moving into apartments of at least two bedrooms in anticipation of children.

But two people I had met recently, Louise and Bobby, didn't fit into any category, and I spent more and more time at their house on 77th Street.

Louise had a wild spirit, while Bobby lived in another world, immersed in Greek literature. One evening he told me he was rewriting *The Iliad*. He worked on Wall Street because he thought he should. Louise had created an exotic setting including huge fish tanks, a swooping white cockatoo, and a house that was perpetually full of visitors—because she could. Huey, the cockatoo, became a metaphor for the household he dominated; free to fly about, he squawked, he flapped, he made surprise landings, especially on women. The fish tanks, overflowing with greens, stood solidly in the middle of the living room, forcing conversations to revolve around them. Louise liked the unkemptness of the greens.

I arrived one morning to hear her yelling into the phone to Bobby's secretary, "He cut the foliage dripping over the tank's top. How could he? It was perfect as it was. When he arrives tell him not to come home. I hate him." Her impulsive, passionate behavior was captivating and magnificent—and very funny.

Louise and I had a provocative friendship, sparking each other's questions on how to claim our confused and unique places in the world. The energy between us was full of fire and in stark contrast to my conversations with most men, who didn't ask my thoughts like Louise did. "Who are you, really? What do you think you want? How much would you dare to get what you want?" Louise saw me as a singular person, and we allowed each other to think outside the rules. I could be attracted to men's power, humor, and sometimes their male ruggedness—and yes, I liked dancing with them. But it was different with Louise. Her impulsiveness was contagious. One rainy afternoon we went to a seedy downtown tattoo parlor and got matching yin-yang tattoos, the complementary balance of opposites, on our inside left ankles. That cemented our friendship.

Years later, the now-faded yin-yang remains a reminder of the potential for balance.

A vision of Louise and our first intimate time together rises dreamily in my memory. In the morning, we could have an hour to ourselves while the baby slept, she had whispered. Her husband would leave at seven for work.

"Here are the keys. You can let yourself in the downstairs door. Come tomorrow, early."

When I arrived at their duplex townhouse, I tiptoed up the carpeted steps to the second-floor front door. We didn't say very much. I eased under the crisp white sheets into the exquisiteness of a passion unknown to me.

Our secret meetings, which lasted for months, would come to an end some day, I knew that. What lay ahead? What price would I have to pay, as Aunt Billie had warned?

"You step onto a path, especially an irregular one, and there's a price," she had said.

The price for discovering a part of me through my relationship with Louise had been worth it.

On a Saturday morning, Louise and I—with Steven, the baby, strapped to her back—stopped at the Central Park Zoo's seal pool. Louise wanted to go inside the zoo, where animals were caged.

"No, I have a sad memory," I said. "I'll wait here."

"What's the memory?" she asked.

"I was little. I stood in front of the beaver's tiny cage, a dirty, uncaring space. The beaver had been given two logs, only two logs, and he sadly—forlornly, really—moved them back and forth. That's all he did," I told her. "It was horrible. I cried. Mother rushed me out to see the seals, 'the fun-loving seals, who do tricks.'"

"Huey has almost the whole apartment to himself, he's free," Louise responded proudly.

I had met Terence before I had gotten to know Louise and Bobby. I had thought about marriage. *One day—if he wants—I'll marry Terence. I like him. He's adventurous, caring, even good-looking. He's divorced, he already has a child and he seems to be a good father.*

My two-week vacation with Terence and a group of friends in Idaho aborted that idea. For a week we rafted down the rapids of the Selway River. The second week Terence and I went off on our own on a four-day horseback camping trip.

He was a good horseman and had a keen sense of the outdoors. We had already been winter camping, which I thought would be freezing and horribly rough, at best. Not at all—a heater, a tiny cook stove, and heavy sleeping bags had made the adventure almost a pleasant one. I liked Terence as a provider, a protector. We had carried our skis up the steep New Hampshire slope, or rather, he had carried all of them after I fell backwards from the weight of my equipment. Instead of mocking me, he laughed with me, and then added my heavy boots to his pack.

It was the same on that summertime trip: he provided, he protected, and we needed each other, especially when the directions to the high mountain lakes for trout fishing baffled me, or when my perfect, small fires proved better than his camp stoves. All went well on that stretch.

But on our way to the airport—he to fly home to Boston, me to New York—we stopped for drinks at a small cowboy bar. We were in good spirits. But after a few cocktails I began pushing our adventure into the past. I was ready to go back to New York, to my friends, to what I perceived as my no-need-to-explain life.

When Terence asked, "What shall we do next weekend? Do you want to come to Boston?" Answers raced through my head. *No, I don't want to plan. I like that you live in another city. Please don't have expectations; I can't fulfill them. I don't want to be a wife. Do I look like a wife?*

I made feeble excuses.

"My parents, I have to stay in New York for the weekend."

"I'll come to New York."

"No, not right away."

It wasn't really his fault. Terence had been kind, patient even. I'm sure had I queried why he didn't ask more questions about my feelings or thoughts, he would have answered me with care, said that he thought he knew me, that he wasn't very good at going deep.

But at that point I had a clear vision of what marriage would mean for me. I would be stuck, always the demure woman behind the man—patient, devoted, listening ... and sold out. Another truth: I didn't want intimacy with Terence.

I wasn't attracted. Once in a while I had a desire, but on my own terms. And I knew this relationship could never be on my own terms.

Poor Terence, sitting there thinking all was going well, not seeing my frustration rising into anger. Confused, I took out my wrath on him.

"Terence, I love a woman," I blurted out.

He stared at me.

"What did you say? Love? A woman?"

I remember him leaning back in his chair, balancing precariously on its back two legs—maybe to get away from me. I remember because I was sure his big frame would break the chair into pieces. It was the same feeling I had as he entered my apartment in New York—the frame of the front door seemed to come in with him, and I felt shoved back into the living room.

He drew in a big breath, a gasp, really.

"You can't. We're together. We've just spent two weeks ... together. We had a good time." His face flushed. His anger rose. "What are you saying? Why are you doing this to me?"

"I'm not doing anything. And it's not to you," I answered, my voice also getting louder. "But it's true."

Terence could be bad-tempered. He stood up. He was so large.

But his rage was impotent. After all, what can a man really do about an unknown enemy? He was boxing without an opponent. His words became explosive. Beer drinkers turned to hear him spit out, "A woman!"

He didn't ask why—just with whom.

"Louise," I said.

"She's married!"

"Yes, she's married," I calmly answered.

Finally Terence threw chilling words at me that couldn't have been more final, threatening my very soul and identity—and giving me an easy exit.

"Some day someone's going to tame you."

"That will never happen," I spat back at him with pent-up fury.

It was over with Terence, and soon the romance would be over with Louise, too.

12

The Amazon

I looked for an escape—from the after-effects of Louise and Terence, my uninspiring job. With the illusion of finding answers in other places, I departed on a three-month hitchhiking adventure through South America. In 1971 Colombia was a relatively peaceful and alluring country. I started my journey there.

I flew into the capital, Bogotá, and went directly to Medellín to meet friends who were leaving for Brazil in a few days. After that I would be on my own, and I was determined to start my hitching experience, even though I knew I would also be taking buses at times. I had been told that Colombian people had a curiosity for foreigners and especially liked practicing their English.

"You'll join other travelers; you'll be fine," my friends reassured me.

I put on what would become my uniform: blue jeans, a long-sleeved black shirt, and brown suede walking shoes, all passable for possible dressier moments. My friends dropped me off at a good spot for catching a ride a few hours' drive south of Medellín. With low-level trepidation I picked up my two lightweight satchels and began. The bags balanced each other as I walked resolutely down the country road toward Bogotá. One contained photographic chemicals and darkroom equipment to be used along the journey. The other held items of clothing—adequate, I hoped, for any occasion, any invitation. Three books completed my luggage: *Spanish Language and Grammar Made Simple*; *The South American Handbook* (then the bible for traveling the continent); and Peter Matthiessen's *At Play in the Fields of the Lord*, which I had finished on the plane and hoped to exchange in an English-language library somewhere soon.

An old blue sedan driven by an elderly woman slowed to a stop almost immediately. This isn't so difficult, I thought. A few miles outside of Bogotá, the road turned and my ride ended. I started walking again, another car soon stopped, and the middle-aged woman driver intimated with hand gestures—her thumb pointing downward—that the location was dangerous.

"Entra, vamos, taxi allí," she said, pointing up the road. Grateful, I got in for the short ride. She told the driver at the taxi stand to take me to a small hotel that had her approval.

Once settled in Bogotá, I called Bill Stevens, an American man who was a friend of a friend in New York. He had lived in Bogotá for years and had created several businesses there. Bill wanted to meet and asked if I played tennis. An odd question, I thought, but I agreed to meet him the next day at La Princesa, my hotel, which Bill nervously described as a "call-girl hotel" when we met the next afternoon. I laughed and told him that explained the price of the room and the corridor noise I'd heard the night before.

Of course I didn't have a tennis racket or the correct clothes.

"No problem," Bill said. "I'll make sure there are some nice choices for you at my club. You'll like it there, a few courts and beautiful gardens, not far from town."

I assumed this would be a friendly game of doubles with another couple. But in addition to the other players, two tennis "assistants" waited for us: a ball boy and a point caller.

"Why do we need a point caller?" I asked Bill.

"Because everyone cheats in Colombia," Bill answered, "so we solve the problem before it starts."

I looked at the couple; they seemed like nice people, not cheaters. Guillermo was friendly and asked about my travel plans and what I thought of his country. Sonia—quiet, like most Colombian women I had met so far—said her English wasn't good enough for conversation but she would like to help me if I needed anything. Perhaps Bill was the cheater, although his appearance suggested a sense of propriety. Slightly gaunt with a bit of a frown on his brow, he seemed older than the forty years he claimed.

Afterward, Guillermo suggested we play again another time.

"Yes, we'll play again," Bill responded assertively, giving me a nod. I wondered if Bill wanted them to think I was his girlfriend.

I mentioned to Bill that I also liked golf.

"No problem."

He quickly arranged for me to play with the female golf champion of Colombia, which terrified me. She and I met the following day at a course near the city. A choice of golf shoes awaited me. The day was beautiful, but our lack of sufficient language skills and her superior golf skill produced a high anxiety afternoon for me. Later, I realized I had been shouting out, "Courage!" when I meant "Great shot!"

No problem, no problem; with Bill as my powerful arranger and re-arranger, everything could be fixed. An ambitious young American, he had come to Colombia in the 1960s to make his fortune. Since his arrival, he had made and lost several, but in the process had secured a place for himself in the Colombian business world. One night in a movie theater, he leaned over during the news and proudly whispered, "I've bribed every politician on that screen."

I considered the difference between his power and those of the young men I knew in New York. Because he had arrived with money, his arena of influence was substantial. And he seemed to be the type of person who took risks in a way my friends didn't. But perhaps they simply hadn't yet developed their shadier, more aggressive sides.

Even though his life intrigued me, and even though he was company—even good company at times—I didn't relish our conversations as I did those I'd had with Louise, conversations that were rich and full of questions—albeit some foolish ones—but which had led to new thoughts. And Bill didn't laugh much.

I wasn't enamored of or physically attracted to Bill, but I envied his ability to navigate a foreign country and cross boundaries—many of which were closed to a woman, a fact I of course weighed with resentment. Bill was a loner, awkward, lanky, plain-looking, lacking in vanity. Yet he also had noticeable good qualities: a persuasive presence, keen eyes that looked directly at a person, and the willingness to listen. I appreciated his deep connection to his adopted country.

He liked Colombians and spoke Spanish fluently. He seemed popular with his workers, although he exhibited the self-indulgence that comes with power. He also had a certain vulnerability that was appealing—for a while. And as I traveled alone, I felt grateful to have a person—particularly a powerful person—to call upon.

Clearly proud of his success, Bill asked me to photograph his diverse projects for a business catalog. Not wanting to miss this opportunity, I relished the days spent photographing: climbing his oil wells, exploring his fiberglass factory, focusing on the people in his hat-making plant who made the ubiquitous rabbit-fur bowlers for the Bolivian peasants. We flew to these places in his refurbished B-29 bomber—an exciting, if uncomfortable ride. Bill worked hard and seemed to have a lucky streak. On a morning walk together down the street in a factory town, he bought a lottery ticket. Three days later, his office received a notice that he'd won—not a lot of money, but enough for a Colombian farmer to buy new seeds for the next harvest. He gestured to the office manager that the winnings were to be divided up among the workers.

I mused about his attraction to me. Despite his success, Bill was surrounded only by business colleagues, not people who seemed like genuine friends. I imagined he saw me as a willing if temporary adventure companion—and perhaps a potential wife.

I also liked being alone in Bogotá. I walked the city. I sat in farmers' market booths tasting *ajiaco*, their beloved potato and shredded chicken soup, and ate the curd-and-bean fried *buñuelos*. My Spanish greatly improved. Some farmers nodded at me as I became a regular with my camera. One morning I stared at a handicapped child and her adoring father. He sang to her and to the passersby, often picking her up, kissing her and putting her back down on her blanket in a new location, perhaps a better one for receiving a few coins. I asked him if for payment I could photograph them for a day or two as we made our way through the market. The father introduced me to vendors and to the local food, expanding my visitor's view of Colombia. The man's pride in our small friendship allowed me into his relationship with his child, giving my photographs an intimacy.

For a few weeks, the city became my center and Bill my anchor. I felt his attentions veering toward the romantic, even though I gave no invitation. One night at dinner he talked about his future and the possibility of children.

"I like Colombia. And the Colombians like Americans. It's a great place to raise a family." He waited for an enthusiastic response.

The day before I left Bogotá, we drove into the lush countryside. Turning off onto a narrow, flower-lined lane of sweet-smelling crown of thorns and *maracuyà*, the climbing passion fruit plant, we stopped, opened all the car windows, and breathed in a paradise of intoxicating scents. Almost overcome, I sighed.

"What a place, a piece of heaven. This road, that charming tumbledown house over there, all in the midst of this wild fragrance. Imagine!"

A farmer passed. Bill called out and asked him if there was land for sale nearby. No land, but he pointed to the house I had spied and said simply, "Se vende."

With a flash of a smile, Bill said, "Let's just see if the owner is there."

We knocked and an elderly man asked us to come in. Yes, he told us, he had grown up in the house, but it now must be sold. As we started the house tour, I trailed the two of them for a while, but I longed to enter my own fantasy. I lingered at the rickety door that gave out to the gardens and took in the trees filled with green and yellow parakeets singing their trill. I walked down paths of giant bougainvillea bushes and took off my shoes to feel the dark brown soil, so fertile it could surely produce flowers and vegetables almost instantly from any seed. In the middle of the lushness stood a gazebo with a worn-out hammock swaying in the scented breeze. As I tiptoed over for a brief hammock swing, I daydreamed that the garden waited for a spade in my willing hand.

Inside, the house contained the same magic: rustic tile floors, slightly crumbling columns that shed specks of green paint and held up a ceiling decorated with angels. A watercolor of the gazebo in a handmade frame was hanging slightly askew from a drooping nail. I could feel an echo of past good moments pervading the house.

Bill called out from the kitchen to come join the owner and him at a table. He waved a piece of paper. It hadn't taken him more than an hour to discuss the sale and put down deposit money. Wide-eyed, I was shocked by his ability and ease to play out his imagination's fantasy. It was one more example of his "no problem" attitude—*I like it, so I'll buy it.*

He and the owner looked at me, both beaming.

"I'll tell you everything," Bill said. "I'll explain. Let's get in the car."

Back on the beautiful dirt lane, we sat for a moment, Bill catching his breath. He darted awkward glances at me.

"This is what I want to say," he said.

"Yes, please, I'm in awe, what are you thinking?"

"I know you're leaving tomorrow for the Amazon and then going farther south. Maybe you won't get back here, so I'll say this now."

"Yes, tomorrow, I'm leaving," I hesitated. "No, I don't believe I'll be back."

Then Bill blurted out, "I want you to know that this house would be yours, your very own, if you would stay."

I stared at him, rattled with disbelief, but also surprised at the unexpected excitement racing through me.

"What?" was the only word I could utter.

"You'll tire of your wandering life, I'm sure. Why not remain here in Colombia?" he asked, waving his hand toward the house. He hardly looked at me, but I recognized the determination in his voice.

I yearned to get out of the car. But the longing to escape was mixed with a lulling thrill as my interior voice repeated jumbled thoughts. *This could be mine? This could be my life? Is that what he said?* Images arose: vivid floral colors, garden scents, men in white linen suits, women in wide skirts with dark flowing hair swaying to the rhythm of the *compás* dance. Old movie images spun in my head.

I spoke softly but breathlessly with a nervous laugh.

"Thank you, I'm appreciative—but well, I don't even know what you mean. What do you mean, Bill? I can't do that. I'm not able to stay here."

Cautiously affronted, part of me wanted to say, *You must be kidding, I don't want to stay here, I have no desire for a life like yours.* But the words remained stuck in my throat. I was suffocating. I felt I knew what he was thinking: I need a wife. No problem, here's an American package who might even be a good one. I'll give her this property. She'll like it here, she'll like me, she'll look good on my arm.

My emotions were tangled. After all, the world of my upbringing honored the opportunity of his seductive offer of a safe, cared-for existence in a beautiful place. A good offer, they would say, even a lucky one. And in the short time that I had been there, I had come to like this culture, their language, their food, the look of the people.

"Are you speaking of marriage, Bill?" I asked a little too loudly. He reached for my hand. I didn't pull back. I told myself to remain calm. After all, Bill had been generous and his hint at our future wasn't entirely unexpected. Having learned the value of soft manipulation, as a woman does, I held his hand and mouthed words of appreciation along with other sentences of pander.

He asked me to think about my life, my future.

Neither rude nor gracious, I answered, "You've been good to me, thoughtful and caring, but now I must return to the hotel. I'm leaving early. Thank you, I'll be all right in Leticia. My friend Katharine, you know, has a job there, it's all okay. And your lab has the films I've taken for you of the projects. The photos are good. We'll talk about it. We'll talk about everything, later."

Bill dropped me at the hotel. We kissed. His wrinkled brow formed the question, *Goodbye?*

My last night. I looked out the window of La Princesa, down onto the street below, watching men in Bogotá's stunning evening light enter the hotel's doors. I smiled, imagining the pleasurable offerings I was told were available in this hotel. It seemed so simple; everyone got what they wanted. Men received sex, women received money. It was a contract that actually was not so far removed from Bill's offer. I would acquire a life, a house, a wealthy husband, beautiful and appealing surroundings. He would acquire a wife, attractive enough and active in supporting his work, one who would hopefully respect his authority and produce heirs. That would be the exchange; it was a perfect fit for the Magnolia Code.

Bill's offer was provocative. But the fantasy slowly faded, replaced by the old vision of confinement. I thought back to Eddie and the danceless dance. At twelve I had learned that I was to abandon my own needs and defer to the boy's, to Eddie's, needs. Bill's offer was the same; it was a contract that worked for many but wouldn't, couldn't work for me.

The next morning I left La Princesa and boarded the prop plane, dropping myself into the discomfort of the seats lining the interior's sides, designed for moving troops, I was told. Through a small window I watched a man approach to turn the plane's propeller. As I closed my eyes, I gratefully heard the roar of the engine. For three hours, as we flew over the dense green jungle, down into the Amazonian basin to the tiny town of Leticia, I felt a wave of ease and the return of the sensual excitement of escape, of crossing boundaries and meeting cultural "others."

13

Farther South

Leticia—the backwater village created by a fortune-hunting American named Jack—sat squarely on the edge of the Amazon at the juncture of Peru, Brazil and Colombia. A tough and aloof man, he had become a celebrity known as "Jungle Jack," renowned in the area for his survival skills and his success in carving out the new town of Leticia. His business supplied research specimens—mammals, reptiles, fish—for the U.S. pharmaceutical industry. As a sideline, he had made this remote location an exotic tourist destination, providing entertainment that included his ability to fight twenty-foot-long anacondas in the deep muddy water—*drugged* anacondas, I found out later, though the fact hardly lessened the thrashing, disturbing sight. Rumor had it that after he walked through a cage of rattlesnakes, he milked them and drank their venom. No one disputed the stories.

Leticia was evocative of every classic jungle movie. A primitive area deep in the steamy, often forbidding Amazon basin, it was filled with strange, frightening animals and exquisite foliage and birds, along with thrilling, unexpected moments. My friend Katharine had arrived in this new town a few months earlier on a two-year journey down through Africa, then up the continent of South America, by varied modes of transportation. After suffering several jungle illnesses and being nursed back to health by nuns at a convent on the Amazon, Katharine had arrived in Leticia and found a job working in Jack's labs. She and I had formed an enduring friendship as students in Italy and as roommates for a brief time in New York.

After her enthusiastic welcome, she told me how lucky I was, that I had arrived just in time.

"In time for what?" I asked.

"Tomorrow morning you can accompany Carlos and his family to the monkey camp, about eight hours up the river from here. He needs to capture tarantulas. He'll take you with him. This is great luck."

This was not an answer I could have imagined, but Katharine was so thrilled at the prospect—"no one gets to go there, it's beautiful, in the middle of nowhere"—that I revved up my curiosity for the adventure, erasing my urge to respond, "I'm already in the middle of nowhere, I want to stay here, in Leticia." I waited for her to say she would go with me, but no—she was needed in the village specimen laboratories, to take care of the monkeys.

Katharine helped me get the necessary supplies for the journey—cheese, bread, a box of crackers, a flashlight, heavy protective socks, bandages—and the next morning I got on the boat with Carlos, his wife Sylvia and their three children. My camera and film were stowed in a metal box, and we began the baking-hot, slow-moving trip, made almost bearable by the meditative chugging of the motor. I amused them with my Spanish. One sentence Carlos spoke that I understood clearly was that if bitten by an Amazonian tarantula, one would not necessarily die—but would certainly scream all night.

The very dark-skinned, indigenous family in residence at the camp responded to me in a friendly, curious way. I remained curious in return, but was shocked by the sight of one of their five children, who had red hair and freckles. I learned that this extreme scramble of genes was common among Amazonians.

We all stared at each other and they giggled at me. We allowed ourselves to wonder at each other's eating habits, sitting postures, cultural mannerisms. But no one pointed at me, nor I at them, although they did show amazement at my height; I was a good six inches taller than their father. All of us wore American T-shirts, but their khaki shorts were held up by belts made of vines. I wore ankle-length boots; they wore rope sandals. For our four small meals a day we sat in a circle on a large rattan mat. I wanted to feel comfortable reaching into the pile of strange pieces of meat, fish, and vegetables that had been placed in the center, but I didn't.

The camp, a quarter-mile walk from the river's edge, fit tightly into the midst of abundant cecropias and elegant, towering Brazil nut trees. Two huts supplied the family's cramped quarters, one for sleeping, the other for working and cooking.

I hadn't expected my hammock to be so close to the family's space. And I hadn't known that my clothes-changing area, on the boat, would be next to the steady pile-up of small tarantula cages. At night I shined my flashlight on that side of the boat for fear of any loose creatures and to calculate the sum of Carlos' quota. Once he had caught 100 tarantulas, I had learned, we could return to Leticia, a now appealing idea. After a few days, the jungle had begun to encroach on me like a humid blanket. I felt trapped, unable to go alone down the indistinct paths because of animal dangers. I was dependent on the others for my safety and for any adventure.

I should have brought more than one book.

But I remember a sublime day. The two boatmen said to come with them. The pirogue slipped quietly away from the shore into the high reeds of the Amazon. Built to navigate the narrowest tributaries, this tiny boat could hardly hold the three of us—two natives with heart-shaped oars kneeling in the front and back, me in the middle. Small, sleek grey dolphins nibbled at my fingertips as I trailed my hands in the lukewarm water.

Even though my shirt stuck to my ribs in the wet heat, I felt ecstatic to be on the river, away from the stultifying camp. The paddling was slow. The headman took his time maneuvering the grasses. He snapped small twigs as reminders for our trip back through the myriad turns of the tributary's maze. He must know what he's doing, I mused.

I wished to go out in the pirogue again, but everyone was busy—Carlos laying traps with his seductive potions in big green leaves, the others hunting. The mother was amused as I photographed her tasks. Black-and-white images of the tarantulas slowly became winning subjects. Part of each day I sat by the river's edge in a clearing designated safe from snakes, where I trained my camera on the extraordinary vegetation.

I was restless. I scanned my mental resources for escape routes but found none. How did this happen? As a child in my cowboy days, as Cactus Pete, I had run from the bad guys, making it across the river, fleeing from any enemy. Now I was stuck, helpless. I knew I should resign myself to my plight, but I couldn't overcome my restlessness. Being trapped focused my thinking on the fleeing I had been doing for the last several years.

One early afternoon on the sixth day, luck arrived. Hearing a seaplane approaching, I ran down to the shore. Matt, brother of Jack, landed and stepped down from the tiny plane. I had met him briefly the evening I arrived in Leticia. His easy presence—tan and strong-looking in his khaki shirt and pants—now seemed even better than I remembered as I calculated my approach to maneuver a plane ride back to Leticia.

After words of greeting, my tone becoming urgent, I said, "Matt, I need to return with you."

"I'm sorry, you can't," he said, astonishing me. "I'm not able to get back up here for two weeks." He turned to the plane's small interior to pull out a pile of mail and boxes of medicines. "Many hunters are arriving soon. I need to plan their trips. The plane is full of all this stuff to deliver. Anyway, you might make too much weight. I have to get going."

"No, I must go with you," I said forcefully. "I'll help you deliver these things. I can't stay here any longer. It's great, it's beautiful, but I'm trapped. Matt, please." My voice took on a pleading tone as I put my hand on his arm.

His hesitation was deliberate. Eyeing my hand, he turned with a cocked eye.

"I don't know. Well…maybe. You're pretty thin, wouldn't overload things too much, I suppose." He laughed. "We could land in Leticia by six tonight." He fiddled with the boxes, and quietly but firmly said, "Then we'll have a drink."

There it was, the signal of the cost of this or other favors. But a quick romance with Matt would be a valid price to pay, maybe even a fun one. He had a sparkle; I'd seen his rugged look on his motorcycle, wheeling down the town's dirt road.

I hadn't used Bill, although he accused me of it in a letter sent a month after I returned to New York. Neither were Matt and I planning to use each other as we stood next to the plane, the motor running. We simply had made a consensual if unspoken agreement—for a few hours' delight, like the ones I had imagined at Hotel La Princesa. There's always a price to pay, as Aunt Billie had told me so long ago.

"Just remember there are consequences, Joanie," she'd said with an amused laugh. "But often it's worth it."

"Yes, we'll have a drink, I'll get my things and say goodbye, I'll be quick," I answered my rescuer.

I squeezed my body in with the plane's supplies. Our three brief touchdowns farther up the river offered different views of the Amazon's beauty; the wildness appeared less threatening. Now, beyond the suffocation of the massive trees, in a plane far above the water, I could see and feel the river's languid, steady power, in step with the jungle.

Returning to Leticia, I found Katharine and told her I was having a drink with Matt. She gave me a knowing look and said how fortunate it was that my escape bargain had included such a good-looking man. Matt and I had several rum-and-something drinks and sat wobbly entwined on his motorcycle, thinking about moving toward his room. But his brother interrupted; a messenger brought an urgent command for Matt to leave for Miami that very night. I learned years later that the majority of their business was sending massive amounts of cocaine, hidden in tree trunks, to Florida. Matt left. I never saw him again. I liked him and would have enjoyed him that night, but the outcome was okay with me. Now I could find Katharine in the village café and exchange stories.

For my remaining ten days in Leticia, in the early morning before Katharine's work began, we spent time leaning on the nets and crates at the river's dock, just watching the supplies come in. Images of *The African Queen* came to mind—the sound of the sputtering engines, the slap of the water exaggerating the river's sultry mood, rickety old boats with paint peeling off. The dock—a muddy, ugly area with a flock of resident vultures—was far from the calm beauty I had witnessed on the monkey camp's tributary. We watched the hated birds of prey swooping and picking at discarded pieces of garbage. I stared at their grace as they soared on the hot wind currents, and saw they had a beauty I hadn't before perceived. Katharine told me that if you can see beyond the fright of the jungle, everything in it has a beauty. There is an underlying paradox of seduction and danger, I remember her saying, "because survival is urgent, choices are quick, without much questioning." I had heard about the woman who was pardoned for killing her baby because she was too weak to breast feed, and about the white men who had been killed by Amazonian Indians because they looked like aliens. Such tales were told in a matter-of-fact way by one of Jack's guides. I learned a bit about the tenuous way of life in the Amazon, just how provisional it was—and paradoxically, that uncertainty helped me think that I could take more risks, believe more strongly in myself.

Katharine wanted to stay on to work in the labs for another year. Although her job had a romantic side, I had seen her distressed look when giving injections to fifty screeching monkeys, but she was determined. I could imagine her staying, but after two weeks in that awkward paradise, I longed to find open space. I flew out of the Amazon on the same prop plane I had come in on, and continued farther south.

Traveling south from Colombia, my connections to travelers, places and cultures, my anxieties and good surprises, were abundant but scattered. Two moments stand out. One was a yearning to belong to an intriguing house in an exquisite orchard—a house similar to the one outside Bogotá—that I spied one soft evening from a slow-moving train near Lima. On that particular evening I felt lonely, and the lovely warm home fed my illusion of safety.

The other was a profound moment of enlightenment on a small Ecuadorian highway ... the truck abruptly drove off.

With three Brazilian journalists, I stood on the side of the road just outside of Guayaquil in a drizzling rain, our hitchhiking thumbs outstretched, hoping for a ride to Quito. A truck stopped. The three men threw themselves and our satchels up into the back of the semi-detached rear cab of the rusted green vehicle. But before the men could pull me aboard, the truck drove off. The license plate slowly faded from view, leaving me engulfed by the smell of cheap gasoline. I heard the men yelling at the driver to stop, but to no avail.

All my possessions, including my identity papers, were on the truck. Without the assurance of a U.S. passport telling the world I was American, a twenty-seven-year-old white woman with visas, I fell into a deep panic. Adding to the absence of clothes and papers was the loss of my camera and undeveloped film, proof of one of my traveling purposes. I felt naked, lost, trapped, and vulnerable. Along with my anxiety, I sat down on a big moss rock. The drizzle turned into a downpour.

But the despair of losing the symbols of my identity wasn't a new experience, I realize now. I had accumulated numerous sufferings of self-doubt. Self doubt, learning to lean on my rebellious bravado and my practiced persona, providing a courageous, if bent crutch with which to lead. I had not yet built inner values strong enough to sustain me in such moments.

But something happened on that road. As I pushed myself up from the rock and began walking, I felt the miracle of grace accompanying me. I was allowed a glimpse into the core of my instinctual self-confidence, so much more powerful than the false promise of my persona. Even without my passport and possessions, I had all I needed, I realized.

I have read that when in despair, one needs to take back parts of oneself. I didn't know it, that day on the road, but those parts I needed to regain belonged to the feisty me—the part of me who was Cactus Pete, full of determination to be myself—even though I didn't then know what that meant. Cactus was in my core, walking with me down the road.

I was afraid this awakening was an illusion and I questioned whether it was just another variation of false bravado. In any case, an ease of self-affirmation arose, and I held on tight.

After about an hour the lumbering truck returned to find me still walking. I grabbed the outstretched hands and climbed into the truck's back cab.

A few weeks later, while staying in a small inn in the town of Cuzco, I felt the damp seep into my room on the eve before I was to take a mountainous train ride into Bolivia. The growing cold influenced my decision to end my trip. I would take the train to Lima and fly on to New York. I wouldn't stop to see Bill; that fantasy was over. If I had been irresponsible or misleading with him, I was sorry, but I didn't feel guilty. I stood at my window, watching the Cuzco peasants gather their unsold goods into colorful blankets. They all wore rabbit-fur bowler hats—probably made in Bill's factory.

The trip had lasted nearly three months. I put my camera equipment into one of my two bags, light now with only the weight of many exposed film cartridges. My belongings went into the other, the treasured *South American Handbook* now placed at the bottom, under my weary clothes.

The miracle of grace on the Ecuadorian road stayed with me. On return to the city, I entered New York University to study social work and basic law. It was so different from my junior college experience ten years prior; I now truly felt the excitement of learning cultural patterns and social systems. NYU was deeply inspiring. The diversity of students supported my desire to understand myriad ways of thinking.

An intimidating course was the drama class, in which students were pitted against each other to answer questions, and since it was the seventies, racial issues were often a dominant theme. A black woman and I were asked to stand in the middle of a circle of white and black students to explain our feelings about the Black Panthers. With our hands jammed nervously in our pockets, we looked out at the audience, avoiding each other's eyes. Rose spoke first and quietly put forth her feelings about white oppression. I hesitated, then answered as best I could: that I had been brought up by Southerners who would not accept their legacy of slavery, that even though I hadn't understood the horror of the term "Jim Crow" in my youth, I knew it was wrong. I told the class that I would never truly understand the depth of racism. A positive response came from a classmate, a black minister, telling me to value my honest confusion. This was one of the paradoxes that I was just beginning to accept. It was not only possible but also desirable to hold two vastly different ideas at the same time. I had to accept the injustice of my background, but part of me still appreciated my Southern roots. And I didn't have to understand the contradictions.

I felt proud that I finished first in my class.

14

Don't Get Caught

After attending New York University, I went to work for a public interest group. I took pride in my work, which showed off my shaky but determined liberal standing, so different from my parents' values. Still, my father supported me by helping to persuade corporate executives to attend the informational meetings I organized.

Father stepped into my apartment on 48th Street between Lexington and Third Avenues.

I gave him a brush of a hug and a quick kiss.

"Shall I make you a scotch?"

"Yes, thanks, Joanie, I'd like a scotch, with soda if you have it."

He laid his coat over the armchair across from the tufted linen couch Mother had recently bought for me at auction. I saw him take in the room: the working fireplace, the green-and-white striped rug I'd found at a secondhand store, the binoculars sitting on the sill for spying across the seventy-five-foot courtyard into other apartments, and the dining room table for four (or a squeezed-in five) by the window.

I had put up a dartboard above the table between the windows, but taken it down for Father's visit. Before his arrival, I thought I'd given the room a careful once-over, but now I saw a glaring darts-casualty crack in one of the window-panes. I could have hidden that by pulling the curtain.

"This is a nice place, Joanie." He looked at me with a smile and gave a brief glance at his watch. "I can't stay too long, but I'm glad you asked me to stop by." He was waiting for me to bring up the subject. I was nervous.

"You were upset that my friend, Bobby Parker, stayed here before he went to South America," I began.

"Before we get into that, how's your job?" He sat down on the other armchair. "I enjoyed going to the lunch you organized the other day. Your director, Joanna, she's interesting."

"I'm really happy you liked the talk. Joanna is so smart, don't you think?" I proudly asked him.

"And she's very good-looking," he added.

I bristled. "Yes, she is, but she's smarter than just pretty." I puffed the pillows, while adding, "We're about to expose a big land fraud in Colorado."

Father

"That's very impressive. Now tell me about Bobby, and why he stayed here."

"Okay, yes, I want to." I moved toward the kitchen to make his drink. I had rehearsed my speech, but now, as I mixed his scotch and soda, I searched for the words.

Returning to the living room, I handed him his glass and sat on the couch, pushing away the two cats, whose destruction of the inset buttons embarrassed me.

"Bobby's my friend, and he was leaving the next day, for a year—a long time." I paused a moment to feel his reaction. "Bobby wanted to tell me about his work in the Amazon. I've been there and he wanted my thoughts. He was anxious, and needed a place to stay for just one night. I wasn't doing anything wrong." I heard my emphasis on the word wrong and knew I'd said it with a whine.

Father sat poised on the edge of the chair, dressed in his dark grey business suit. I assumed his silk socks were held up tight by the hidden garters that had fascinated me as a child. I considered his boyish handsomeness, his soft hair and red cheeks, and imagined him reflecting on my phrase "not doing anything wrong."

"Joanie, I want to tell you this. It just doesn't look right. You can't have boys staying in your apartment. People will talk about you." Holding his drink on his knee, he said with a slight plea, "You're not married. I wish you could understand. And it's not that I'm mad," he said. He hesitated and looked down as if to make sure his shoes had held the polish.

"I'm disappointed."

That dreaded word.

"Disappointed? In what?" I heard my voice rising. "And who's going to talk about me, the doorman?" I asked with sarcasm. "Nothing happened."

Father leaned toward me and answered firmly and quickly.

"The point is not if anything happened. It's how it looks. I trust you, Cactus, but you could get a reputation." He stopped and took a big swallow of his drink. Then, more quietly, he said, "You should understand that there are ways of living this life, and your life is a good one." He paused; I saw a slight frown furrow his forehead.

"You've had, and you have, every opportunity. Don't open yourself up for people's judgments by making bad choices." He jiggled the ice and took another gulp. His face had reddened a bit. "What I'm saying, Joanie, is don't mess up. I can't be more plain."

"What do you mean, mess up?"

Father left my question hanging. He got up and made himself another scotch. On the way out of the kitchen he stopped at the window and raised the binoculars to see what was going on in the lit-up room across the way. The apartments were just close enough to spark one's imagination; it was like living in Hitchcock's *Rear Window*. He put the binoculars down with a small laugh.

Unconsciously he let his finger stir the ice in his refreshed drink, and with a soft yet serious look said, "I'm going to tell you something I probably shouldn't." He paused and took a sip. "It's not for a father to say this to his daughter. But I will. I will because it's important and because I love you. This is what I came here to say: Do what you want in life, but Joanie, don't get caught. You're daring, you have a lot of spunk and you could get in trouble. There are rules in life. There's decorum. Be careful."

I remained quiet and pulled at the couch buttons' loose threads. I didn't look up at him, but I perceived an unease, or perhaps he, too, heard the injustice in his words of male entitlement. After all, he did have three daughters, and all of us, in one way or another, had to maneuver in a man's world. But two daughters were already safely married—or so he imagined. It was me who posed the potential trouble. "Don't get caught" was a warning, a thoughtful warning. For a moment I thought he was on my side.

But he broke the rules all the time with his constant flirtations, his other life. Men could "mess up" in my parent's 1970s world without much consequence. "But he always comes home to me," Mother often said, appeasing herself with his tossed crumbs. Her longing for him could be called pitiful— with the Southern-drawl emphasis on the word pitiful.

"Do you believe in the double standard?" I blurted. "I mean would you be saying this to a son?" I felt a flush coming to my cheeks. I hadn't made myself a drink, but now I wanted one just to put the cool against my face.

"I would say it differently; boys, men, are different. We work hard, we have a lot to think about in order to provide for a good family life. And," he uttered as he fumbled for his back-pocket handkerchief, "men have needs that are different from women's; that's just the truth of it. We're allowed leeway." He leaned away from me.

"Do you know what I mean?"

"Not really," I mumbled, wondering how we could cross our father-daughter gap. I doubted we ever could.

Father nervously adjusted the knot in his tie, and continued.

"But women, nice women, their lives can be ruined by stepping over the line. 'Damaged goods,' someone once said about a young girl I knew in the office."

I wondered if it was he who had damaged the goods.

He blushed, clearing his throat.

"Women should have high standards. Girls are born to do other things, other tasks, important tasks: create a place in society for their family, for themselves, work for the good of others and," he emphasized, "be respected." He looked into his drink. "Look at your mother. She's a good example of decorum."

My rising anger made me itch. Scratching my arm, I said sharply, "But Mother's not a happy person. I mean do you actually think she's happy? She waits for you. All the time, she's just...." I could hardly say it. "Waiting."

Father got up. "I have to go," he blurted out. "I'm having a drink with a business acquaintance. I'm late." His eyes were darting; he looked irritated and anxious to leave. I of course didn't ask him who the "business acquaintance" was. I didn't want to catch him in a lie. But my silence hinted at my guess.

I felt calm. I'd been brave but not belligerent. I'd been truthful. I rose from the couch to say goodbye.

Father quickly put on his coat. He stopped at the front door and turned to me.

"What about that nice man, Edwin Phillips? He wants to marry you. Why not him? He's upstanding, has a nice job." Buttoning his coat slowly, he added, "Good looking man, too. You once told me you had fun together. Yes, why not, you should marry Edwin," he pronounced somewhat lightly. A last thought occurred to him, "And Joanie, he would always be there on Saturday nights."

It took me a few seconds to register his comment.

"Yes, Edwin's a nice man and you're right, he would be there on Saturday nights." I stared at Father, willing him to really see me. "But I wouldn't be."

He didn't speak, but his eyes narrowed into a penetrating stare. Slowly he shook his head. But after a moment—which seemed an eternity—a smile started on his playful face. With a grin and a slight chuckle, he pulled me toward him and gave me a loving hug. I heard his laugh as the elevator door closed.

15

Nadia

I looked down the long, straight flight of stairs as I left our friend's loft in New York's Little Italy. At the bottom of the steps the door was open to the street. Nadia stood on the sidewalk, waiting. Darkness surrounded her, but a sliver of light from the street lamp illuminated one side of her face. She looked up the stairway, and seeing me, she lifted a corner of her black cashmere shawl to just under her black eyes. This beautiful, Arab-world gesture was so much a part of her—an Egyptian woman—and it drew me under her spell.

Our intense but somewhat careless relationship started in 1977. My desire to cross cultural boundaries, see and hear a diversity of faces and languages, plus my entrance into the fascinating world of the United Nations, where she worked, were all realized through Nadia. Yet at the same time our relationship propelled me backward into a lack of self-worth. Choice and consequence and a price to pay, just as Aunt Billie had said. All were wrapped up in this liaison, which continued on and off for years. Still, I do not regret it. In fact, the price for that heart-hurting experience helped push me down the path toward self-appreciation.

Nadia and I met through our mutual friend, Joe, a filmmaker brought up in New York's Greenwich Village who seemed to know everyone of any nationality. She and I had an immediate attraction; both of us laughed at anything remotely funny, and each found the other exotic in a way. Our meetings in the night were intensely intimate but with no further commitment. I moved into her apartment, I moved out and back to mine, then into hers again.

Occasionally others lived in her second bedroom. Joe was there for several months. Some wandering friends, like Gino, or Nadia's cousins, would stay for three or four weeks at a time.

Parties were frequent. Nadia's Egyptian friends, my friend's, Joe's—anyone, everyone came—even a member of Osama Bin Laden's family showed up. Someone once called Nadia's apartment the "powder room at Port Said." Drugs and liquor flowed; the music was loud. Other apartment owners did not contain their anger at the noise and chaos of the comings and goings in the small, carefully landscaped building on 51st Street and the East River. For the most part, we ignored them. We invited one upstairs neighbor to join us, and she stopped complaining.

Nadia was short, much shorter than I, but her bearing, always magnified by high heels, gave her a commanding presence. Her black eyes darted over the crowd through the party haze. Her bejeweled being, her smoky voice, and her enchanting laugh captivated. She danced and sang, she flirted and seduced, she was impossible to capture. I can still picture her sitting on a bar stool in Lynn's Piano Cafe on Lexington Avenue singing *La Vie en Rose* to a room full of enraptured drinkers.

Amazingly, Nadia always arrived at her job exactly on time. The UN was her driving force. She was a rising star and her job as chief of protocol defined her. She practiced an art that at times was an empty seduction game. Her favorite quote was one from Shakespeare's *Antony and Cleopatra*: "She makes hungry where most she satisfies."

My job was not my driving force. Although I cared deeply about the mission of the public interest group, I felt drawn to my photography work more and more.

I visited the UN often. I roamed the halls to listen to the languages and gaze at the splendor of the delegates' dress in the dining room. I asked Nadia endless questions about the Arab world, its authors, its history. At one point, exhausted by my curiosity, she replied, "You are more interested in my people than I am." And, she added with some amusement, "You want to know about my people? I'll tell you. This is what we say: 'Our future? She is behind us.'"

In mid-January, a year after we met, I traveled to Cairo; Nadia would come a few days later. We were to stay at her parents' apartment while they were in Paris for six months on business, an annual exodus. I arrived sick with fever, and my delirious state was heightened by the muezzin's enigmatic call to prayer coming through the bedroom window my first morning. That mesmerizing, long plea of a sound, and the entrance of a very tall man dressed in a black gallabiya uniform, holding a tray of tea and toast, were keys that opened the secret door to an ancient culture. I was reminded of that moment at age eleven when I ran through the normally bolted gates of the Carnegie Mansion. Again I had entered a mysterious world for which the invitation to stay was either not given or merely temporary.

The question that morning—"Tea, toast, Madame?"—penetrated my delirium. The fragrance of strong black tea was appealing and sickening at the same time, but I said yes to the offering to ensure his exotic presence would re-enter my room.

I wandered the spacious apartment, fascinated by the contrast between the interior treasures—two huge elaborate Chinese screens in the living room, Pharaonic figures, and Middle Eastern vases—and the building's graffiti-covered stairway, burned-out light bulbs and broken elevator.

Nadia arrived and for a day or two she showed me the world of old Cairo. We sat on the floor of the acclaimed architect Hassan Fathy's apartment in the ancient dirt-street section of Cairo and sipped cups of mint tea while Fathy explained his philosophy: building with ancient design methods and materials, all with a focus on efficient beauty, the process of which I had read about in his captivating book, *Architecture for the Poor*. I heard a woman sing the music of Om Kalsoum—known as "the Star of the Orient"—in a dusty café on Cairo's outskirts. I smelled the deep scents of spicy kabobs from the sidewalk braziers, and I stared at the crowds in luscious Arab dress—often dirty, but with glittering coins sewn down the front. I had never noticed eyes very much until I saw the dark beauty of Arab eyes. I was intrigued.

Nadia's attention, always fleeting, soon focused on meeting friends and cousins at the Hilton Hotel bar. The bar—minimal, comfortable, and modern—represented the place where contemporary Cairenes came to shed the passé, old-fashioned attitudes of Egypt. I remember many drinks—always scotch—and loud laughs, and most of all my desire to flee from my discomfort, which must have shown on my flushed face. My French was passable but unremarkable. Her friends' excellent English—not their language of choice—and the interspersed Arabic phrases (although not a language in which the upper class was proficient) reinforced my place as the foreigner. The group paid little attention to me. I felt awkward, the superfluous outsider meant simply to witness—along with her entourage—Nadia's cultivated charm. Although I wanted to go to the souk or the extraordinary Museum of Cairo, I didn't have the bravado to extricate myself from that scene of which I was expected to be a part—superfluous or not.

Meeting Nadia's cousin Nayela in Alexandria was an altogether different experience. As we entered her garden, strewn with a circle of chairs awaiting conversation, a very grey-haired, lovely, slightly unkempt woman in her seventies immediately took my hand.

"Come sit by me. I hear you love my country," Nayela said. "I will tell you stories of old Egypt, the days of King Farouk—my cousin married him, you know—the horseback rides by the pyramids, the family orange groves. Yes, leave Nadia's friends over there. Let them talk to one another."

Elated, I implored, "Please, yes, tell me your stories."

"First, here comes Ahmet with our hors d'oeuvres."

Another beautiful, tall, dark-complected male came in carrying a large silver tray. He approached us and, with a slight bow to Nayela, offered an array of perfectly rolled hashish cigarettes laid side by side. My astonished look made Nayela laugh, yet she asked with care, "Oh, perhaps we should just share one. Would that be all right with you?"

I was captivated by her melodious voice as she told the stories I had fantasized. Her laugh was similar to Nadia's, and her tales, especially of Queen

Farida's role as president of the Feminist Union, were told with a cynic's tone that charmed me.

After a week in Cairo, Nadia and I and various cousins and their girlfriends travelled the road to the Kharga and Dakhla oases. We drove south of Cairo and then west across the desert into "the magnificent emptiness," as a Persian friend calls the Sahara. We sped fast to avoid getting stuck in the soft sand, and we poked our heads out the car window, mystified by a man on a camel lurching around and around in a circle in the middle of nowhere.

"Desert madness," a cousin commented.

We stopped for a break in a tiny village and sat on unsteady handmade chairs in a circle on the dirt plaza. A woman came out of her house to ask if we would like tea, the customary gesture of hospitality. Then the woman stopped and looked at me, and said that I looked familiar, that we had met before.

"No, you couldn't have," Nadia answered, understanding the rural Arabic. "She is American, from New York. Do you know where New York is?"

"Yes," she answered proudly. "When planes fly overhead, they fly to New York."

The group looked at the woman and then at me, the only very white person in the circle.

The shy woman repeated with emphasis, "Yes, we have met."

That she connected me to her desert world afforded me a temporary sense of belonging.

Nadia and I weren't known as a couple, not even slightly. The thought of something so serious and blatant might have occasionally occurred to me, but not to her. Her life included liaisons with other women and sometimes men. I pretended that was the way life was, even though her detachment was painful. In fact, I now think of our relationship as a fantasy. And even in the alternative lifestyle of 1970s New York—the raucous chic of Studio 54 and semi-dangerous downtown dance clubs at the beginning of the AIDS epidemic—the importance of façade was key. Authenticity took a back seat, not just for me, but for many friends.

I learned from Nadia's mother, Dodie, for whom I had a great affection, that privileged Egyptians learned to understand life's fragility as a result of Nasser taking over the country in the mid-1950s. To have so much—the splendor of one's own orange groves criss-crossing beautiful landscapes, lovely houses, and a sophisticated job working for King Farouk—and then lose almost all of it overnight created a sense of tenuousness that I knew nothing about. Hearing Dodie's memories affected me. The positive message was to live life with a certain urgency. The negative was to elevate glamour and live for appearances. And of Nadia, I could hear my father's warning: "Joanie, I know you're going to do what you want, but don't get caught."

I had a dreamy fantasy of us out in the desert, tying up our camels, the soft sand gently blowing our way as we enjoyed whatever and took what was given with no responsibility. A person must take responsibility, I knew. But I had not yet reached that level of self-assurance. Instead, I had a longing I couldn't name.

My mother, too, had a longing—for the little full-of-hope Southern girl she had left behind. Aunt Billie had a different kind of longing—to know who she was.

I recognize the core of my longing now in a way I couldn't have then. A Welsh translation for longing is the yearning for "a home that doesn't exist." I yearned for acknowledgment of me as an individual—from others, from society, and especially from my mother.

Surprisingly, Mother eventually gave me the acknowledgment, but not until after she died.

Nadia probably had longings, too. I had seen a loneliness behind her façade. I can visualize our sweet, sensual love in the Paris bedroom, when her depressions made her vulnerable and soft.

But once at home in New York, her façade soon reasserted itself. I remember her appreciative gaze at herself in the mirror after throwing me a deprecating remark, that I was the betrayer.

"Betraying myself is more the case," I threw back.

She hesitated, perhaps appreciating the truth for a moment.

"One day you will slam the door on me, and never come back," she said.

She turned away, ripping the brown paper off the dozen white roses she had brought home. In one hand she held a vase filled with water into which she merely shoved the flowers, as though she felt no need to care for them further.

And she was right. I did leave, although our volatile relationship held a seduction for me until a few years before her death.

Black Mesa, New Mexico

16

Santa Fe

In the fall of 1981 I again exited New York amidst a struggle, this time from the wobbly life with Nadia on 51st Street. I think back to my mother's need to escape our apartment and wonder if I was in some ways following her example, embracing the idea that it was somehow better "out there."

It was meant to be a short break to Santa Fe, New Mexico with Joe to work on research for a film on how Santa Fe's three cultures—Hispanic, Native American, and Anglo—fit and yet didn't fit together, how the cultures comingle, each with distinctions, existing side by side. Our six-month research effort and financing would be undertaken with the guidance of the New Mexico Museum Foundation.

I changed my city shoes to my cowboy boots in the Albuquerque airport. Excited to be in the Southwest culture, I felt a remnant of the soul of Cactus

Pete begin to emerge. Even though I'd been to Santa Fe before, the one-hour drive north felt more enticing than it had during my visit five years prior. The rawness of the desert was no longer forbidding. Instead, the vastness held a mystery; it seemed to be a place where anything could happen. The uncrowded landscape of the high mountain desert felt inspiring.

We arrived on Halloween. It felt auspicious to land in this place where the spirits of the dead were honored on All Hallow's Eve, a good sign.

Some consider Santa Fe a bohemian outpost, a place that draws those who don't fit into a conventional mode, especially artists. While people often refer to Santa Fe as an arts center, it is more a center of creativity. They say the city, as New Mexico's capital, has an attitude and reputation of not quite belonging to the United States. I felt an affinity for both references—that it didn't belong, and that it had attitude.

A week after I arrived I met Emily, a refined, mischievous eighty-year-old woman who had lived in Santa Fe on and off since her thirties, when she arrived with her father from Chicago in his bank's private railcar. Emily was wise and had a wonderfully odd sense of humor. To tease her beloved Native American friends at her birthday celebration—the night I met her—Emily regally wore a headband with half an arrow attached to each side.

Over her one-ample-vodka-a-night, Emily warned that newcomers could stay in Santa Fe only if they meant to be honest.

"Never remain in the closet," she said. "Those who do are sent home." She wasn't referring to being gay; she was simply saying that you must be real, you must risk being true to yourself, whatever the consequences. I could hear Aunt Billie's voice in my head.

Emily and I immediately became friends.

Joe and I, both urbanites, immersed ourselves in what we fantasized was the cowboy world. We thought the whooping and whistling cattle drive we witnessed one day ten miles north of the city was a mirage. Everywhere we turned we encountered another character.

The warning, "Don't go up north to interview the Chicano Ike de Vargas, he's dangerous," only spurred us on. The handsome Ike greeted us on a cold day, and after sweeping off a snow-covered log with his machete, invited us to sit down. If Ike represented a dangerous man, I was enchanted. He was proud to show us the hospital clinic he had started in remote Northern New Mexico. And it was fascinating to hear his stories of the ancient *patron* or Hispanic "mafia" system that still forcefully controlled this small part of the world. "Uncle Emilio," as the *patron* was called, held power over Rio Arriba County, his Northern New Mexico domain. Ike dared to run against him in a local election. He didn't win.

In Santa Fe, eccentricity was applauded and drinking was encouraged. I'm sorry I missed the fights that had spilled out onto Santa Fe's artistic Canyon Road from the infamous Claude's bar. Our new friend Peter, born and bred in Santa Fe, told us how his beautiful mother, after several tequilas, once rode her horse through the front door of La Fonda hotel and ordered drinks for everyone standing. All of this fed my sense that I had landed in the middle of an old Western film.

We interviewed many diverse people for the film and had the good fortune to be invited into houses and ranches of Hispanic and Anglo families and reservation homes of Native Americans. We spent an unforgettable afternoon with Concha Ortiz y Pino, an eighty-year-old state legislator and regal matriarch of the "old Indian bones" village of Galisteo. Charming and tough—she often wore a holstered gun—Concha looked us in the eye as she recounted tales of the three cultures' ability to get along.

"Of course, they had to," she said, clasping her hands together. Concha's hair was pinned in tight rolls at the back of her neck where, I imagined, bullets and cigarettes were hidden. As for Northern New Mexico's traditional Catholic sect known as the Penitentes, Concha answered our mystified question regarding their ritual of self-flagellation simply.

"Well, you diet, don't you?"

The film's research time ended. Our script was written but stored in the archives of the art museum for lack of funds; it was a difficult financial time in general and particularly for the museum foundation.

By then, even though the documentary wasn't produced, I was hooked, drawn to Santa Fe, to what I perceived as a compelling world. I stayed. It is not easy to say why it seemed the right moment to risk a different future, but I was quite sure the decision, though impulsive, was a good one.

I didn't know what to expect, but my first six months were a good omen. I thrived in a town full of believable legends and fascinating people. I met Sarah, who embodied Southern beauty and the South's dark and sensuous sides. She had lived in Santa Fe for ten years before we met and was a highly respected art dealer credited with broadening Santa Fe's art image to include contemporary— not just Western and native—art. After my provocative but negative relationship with Nadia, meeting Sarah was like walking into a room full of breezy air. While she oozed Southern charm, Sarah knew how to escape the stifling side of the Magnolia Code's manners and correctness. The irony is that she would have been my parent's perfect Southern pick for me—except for her gender.

We bought a two-hundred-and-fifty-year-old house in Estaca, thirty-five miles north of Santa Fe, from an opera singer who, rumor had it, sang nude in the garden while guzzling glasses of wine. Although the village of thirteen was only an hour's drive from Santa Fe, it seemed like another country, not only Spanish-speaking but distant in its old-world atmosphere. Most area farmers traveled to Santa Fe just twice a year for supplies. We were told that a hundred years before, our house—which sat next to a small, sweet chapel— had been the community center. Now a traveling priest from nearby San Juan Pueblo offered a homily in Spanish every few weeks. I dreamt I heard the villagers' feet dancing on our forty-foot-long living room floor, which had been created out of the traditional mix of mud, ox blood, and straw. We slept in one of the two tiny bedrooms that had once housed the animals. The kitchen looked out onto an old but nurtured garden and the five-hundred-yard walk down to the Rio Grande, through fields of chiles, had a charm. It was difficult to swim in the swift-running water, where bits of barbed wire and other objects were hidden, but hanging from an overhead branch was a thrill for my dangling legs in the summer heat.

On winter mornings, we ran into the kitchen to light the corner fire. The house's only heat came from its three fireplaces, making winter torturously cold at times, although when the two-foot-wide adobe walls heated up, it became warmish. However, the need to retain the heat in the walls prevented trips away for more than three days.

Perhaps it was the isolation, the village's poverty, the lack of promise, or for us the disconnect from the world, but drinking abounded—for everyone, including Sarah and me. Violence and machismo were the norm. One Saturday noon Sarah and I stopped at Bill's Bar in the nearby tiny village of Mora. A crowd of high-spirited cowboys with money in their pockets filled the musty room. Sarah and I angled ourselves onto bar stools, smoking and engaged in rapt conversation. A drunk man came over, asking for a cigarette. Sarah, usually the epitome of Southern politeness, answered roughly, "No, we're having a deep conversation, can't you see?" The man, stunned by his dismissal, lurched over to the bar's side door and knocked down the first person who entered. The next man landed a punch on another and the fun, the itch to hit someone, erupted; it was as simple as that. Nervously thrilled by the scene and the yells, we crawled out through the maze of cowboy boots.

We became friends with the noisy neighbors across Estaca's dirt road. But their fighting ended badly one Sunday afternoon when she knifed him. She aimed for but missed his heart, and the blade struck him hard in the arm. He in turn hit her in the back with a two-by-four, sending them both—she still yelling at him—to the hospital. Another afternoon Sarah found a neighbor sitting dead in his truck by a beautiful spot along the river. I remember her easy, cynical comment, wondering aloud why he had picked that particularly enchanting location in which to shoot himself.

North of Estaca, farms and ranches spread out all the way up to the Colorado border. A tired terrain prevailed. Some of the houses sagged with the burden of harsh winters, and the horses had a heavy gait, yet there was a great beauty, particularly on the rutted dirt roads going up the back way to Mora. Through the four seasons I photographed a large grove of black walnut trees that had lengthened into a graceful vertical line. Every one or two weeks I drove the nearly two-hour journey to this spot, climbing over the fence with my tripod and camera to sit and wait for the inspiration to enter the mood of this place, so unfamiliar to me. One time a beaten-up truck stopped, which scared me, but the rancher, Roberto, just wanted to chat. Dressed in the soft worn jeans and mud-slung brown jacket uniform of the area, he told me that he, too, often stopped at this place because of his love for the trees.

"What else do you like up here?" he wanted to know. I told him I hoped to photograph the small mission churches. I'd heard about how they anchored the community. Eager to start me on the search, he pointed the way and said not to listen when people said a place wasn't safe.

"Go anyway," he laughed, tipping his beaten-up cowboy hat, "people are kind here, and even though they will think you're an alien, they'll help you." My camera was giving me a further opportunity to cross into another world.

Judith, a soulful still-life painter and friend, wanted to join me on the mission church project, she to paint the church images and I to photograph the spirit of the place. In her go-anywhere Jeep we started down one more dirt road, one that didn't show up on any map. The road wandered, holding the charm of surprising turns and subtle beauties as we meandered through a ranch, across a bridge. Another bend in the road and off to the right were the ruins of old, now-empty farm houses, a large falling-down church, and a building with a roof-top bell that could have been a one-room schoolhouse. An old farmer, a survivor of this village, Concepción, described how his childhood fiesta days centered on the chapel.

"Lots of food, music—good music from José's little squeeze box."

No electricity, but with the help of light streaming through the windows, I took photographs inside some of the small family chapels: a statue of Jesus dressed in a wedding gown hanging on a rough nail; contemporary dolls out-fitted as nuns, angels, or altar boys; broken-down wooden pews. A woman watching over our work asked why I would photograph dolls instead of the paintings of Christ or the dramatic renditions of the crucifixion. I wanted to tell her that I was intrigued by the expression of the local culture, that you would feel comfortable putting a wedding dress on your beloved Jesus figure, an odd

Jesus in a bridal dress, northern New Mexico chapel

sight that I question, but I thought she'd think me rude. Their lives seemed so remote; their spirituality, like everything else, travelled down its own creative path.

Even though most villagers had little income—just their farms—they were generous. A warm spirit and a surprising sense of humor prevailed. A farmer with whom Judith and I had a long conversation answered my "Thanks, how great it was to talk with you," with, "How great it was to look down your shirt." I burst out laughing. We drove off down the shortcut dirt road he had pointed to and nervously hoped he wasn't planning to follow us.

Out of our collaboration of paintings and photographs, Judith and I created a text and image book called *Symbols of Faith*, showing our version of New Mexican beliefs from an outsider's point of view. It became a popular local book that I still spy in libraries and bookstores. I also showed large black-and-white images of the grove of trees in a Santa Fe gallery, and exhibited photographic collages in a New York gallery.

Sarah and I lived an isolated but fascinating rural life on a property everyone wanted to visit for Sunday lunch, even the nearby nuns, who knew they could find a glass of Sunday afternoon wine with us. Life for the year and a half in Estaca was all about our fantasy: Let's live far into the country, some place we don't know, New Mexico foreign. With not much more thought than that, the move from the city had been easy: we just picked up and left, in a why-not moment. This time the risks—to move to and then to exit Estaca—were successful.

I had been an appreciative observer of the world around me, often just as exotic as other cultures, but my curiosity for a rural life like Estaca had been fulfilled. The fantasy had come to an end. We stopped drinking. It felt like a new door was about to open. Sarah and I drifted apart, along different paths— she to get her master's at the University of New Mexico in Albuquerque and me to pursue my photography in Santa Fe. We sold the Estaca house and with thoughtful care, went our separate ways.

A New Mexico Snow   Monotype

An Absence of Essence

17

Essence

Through photographing women, I came to better understand myself and the essence of the feminine.

The spirit of Ramoncita, the aunt of my good friend Mae, was full of generosity.

"She laughs a lot, we love her—and she's ninety," Mae exclaimed.

My photographs of Ramoncita—crocheting on her meticulous porch in the village of La Madera, hovering over tortillas on the ancient stove in the warmth of her kitchen—tell the story. She represented an old-fashioned belief in hospitality and the notion that everything around her mattered. Her big soul filled the camera frame.

The young girl in a Santa Fe mechanic's garage showed similar character, pushing herself underneath the cars on a wheeled dolly with a few swear words, a laugh and a greasy wrench in hand. Beautiful to look at, hair arrayed about her head in an aura, she announced, "If you want a picture, you'd better get under here with me."

Ramoncita

I recognized the determination in the face of the elderly woman at Susie's Roadside Café. As she worked her arthritic fingers to create hour hands out

Doris

Susan

Marion

Mary

of chiles for a battery-operated tortilla clock, she recounted stories of her Hispanic neighbors.

"That poor farmer, he chased his cow until that cow turned on him, really mad, and chased him back to the barn. Carlos was so scared I couldn't help but laugh at him. But one time I heard him weeping behind the barn because he had to kill his favorite pig. I didn't think I liked him much until I heard him crying like that."

Wisdom showed on the face of my then-eighty-year-old friend Susan. People came to her for answers. It didn't seem to matter what the question was; Susan reached into her compassionate core and gave a thoughtful resolution. She had "the quality of daring to answer from the heart—rather than just the mind," my friend Ali said. I caught an image of Susan's concentration as she sat in the sun on her *portal* in Pojoaque.

But I didn't find such amazing women only in New Mexico.

Mary, a sixtyish waitress at Junior's Cheesecake restaurant in Brooklyn, had an attitude that was open and fiercely vulnerable. It took several meetings over coffee to break through her suffer-no-fools veneer. She had spent thirty-five years at Junior's and was planning her retirement in Florida, where she could finally take it easy and leave life's duties behind. With a cigarette dangling from her lips, she described the mostly rotten men she'd loved.

"If only I hadn't spent so much time on my back," she told me one day with a wink. An extremely funny but poignant answer.

The women I met in India held a special fascination for me. Since the age of eighteen I had travelled to that compelling country. In 1998 I made plans with Ali, another India-lover, to return. Ali would work with artisans in several places to create clothing designs. I would photograph women with help from Anand Sarabhai, a new friend I had met in Santa Fe but who lived most of the year in his native Ahmedabad, in the state of Gujarat. Anand helped me contact the Self Employed Women's Association (SEWA), a nonprofit entity established by Mahatma Gandhi and Anand's family. Their reply was enthusiastic; they needed images of SEWA's support for the unprotected female workers and asked if I could produce photographs of the Women's Bank, the artisans, the garbage

Incense roller

workers—all of whom either received loans or, as part of the "untouchable" class (the Dalit), were guaranteed jobs. SEWA would provide me with a car or motorcycle and a guide. I answered with inspired anticipation.

We arrived at the vast garbage dump just outside the city of Ahmedabad at dawn. The sun lit up the pieces of metal, paper, clothing, and other fragments of life thrown onto the heaps of piled rubbish.

I got out of our Indian-made Ambassador car to follow my two non-English-speaking guides, who had been told I wanted to photograph the ragpickers and the garbage dump. Positioned among the piles of trash were twenty or so young women. A few power lines hung overhead; vultures swooped among the hills of garbage. A smoky haze steamed up from the refuse a truck had just emptied. Other than the faint screeching of the birds, it was silent. All the women were bent to their task of stabbing selected items and depositing them in huge white plastic bags slung over their shoulders.

Benares Market Women   Monotype

The Ragpicker

The pickers, aged from approximately twelve to forty, wore all the finery they owned. Treasures were presumed safe, I had heard, only if displayed on their bodies. Care was taken not to tangle their dresses or snag and break a bangle. Saris flowed in the early morning breeze, and hands moved in the graceful Indian gesture of gently pulling the sari material over the top of one's head.

We stopped at the edge of the dump, I with my camera in hand. The pickers looked at me, I looked at them, and they went back to their picking. I kept staring and began the difficult journey of crossing from my world into theirs.

One woman stared back at me. I imagine my guide had told her to look like she was working hard, as she then threw herself into stabbing pieces of garbage with a fury that exceeded dedicated labor. She stopped and turned to me again, miming, *"Look, do you see how hard I'm working?"* My camera

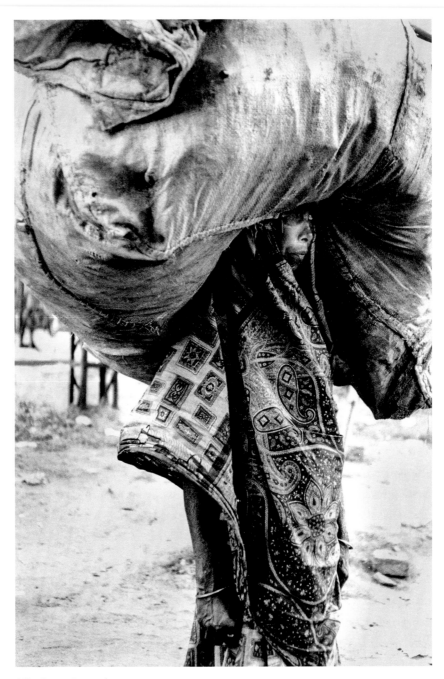

The Street Ragpicker

Women's bank in Ahmedabad

remained poised as we eyed each other for a long moment. Out of the blue, for no reason, an unexpected current of connection flowed between us; our shrugs met in the void. She put her pick down and lifted her hands into the air, gesturing around her, as if to ask, "*Can you believe this mess? What are we doing picking at these scraps?*" I smiled, my own hands in the air, answering in agreement, "*I have no idea.*" She bent over with a laugh and gave me a wave before resuming her job.

She and I were a picture of unassuming opposites, two humans each doing their work—she picking at the discards of her society, making a few rupees a day; I, in my photographer' vest stuffed with film, an extra lens, and a filter or two, wearing an expensive camera around my neck, recording her life. I fantasized talking to her, sitting on top of the garbage piles, enjoying an Indian tea. I wanted to ask her mundane questions—where she lived, how she lived, which pieces of garbage she would consider a prize and why. That she would want to speak to me was perhaps a ludicrous thought, but that's what I would have liked, and for a moment I presumed that she, too, would be willing.

I had hoped to catch the intimacy of that particular exchange, but my images of her were of no consequence. They were poignant and romantic, perhaps, showing her beauty in contrast with the harsh, ugly backdrop, but my self-reflective distraction made me miss the opportunity to describe her reality. Fortunately photographs I made that day of other ragpickers expressed the drudgery of their situation. I was extremely proud that two of my ragpicker photographs were later chosen for a United Nations exhibit, "Progress of the World's Women," including work by sixty female photographers from fifty countries.

On that same trip I visited the Women's Bank in Ahmedabad several times. One Friday a crowd of men filled the bank. I didn't understand why men were there. The surprising—and, to me, fantastic—answer was, "On Fridays men are allowed to put the deposits of their wives' work into their family accounts, but they are not allowed to withdraw any money." This was such a giant leap, the men ceding a measure of financial control to the women. I was shocked. It was hard to imagine how the men had adjusted to this shift.

During a SEWA empowerment workshop, I watched the expression of one woman who stood on a stage and was directed to identify herself. After many halting tries over a period of an hour, and with the help of a SEWA coach, she courageously found her voice.

"Priyanka, she shyly announced, "and not just 'the wife of' ... "

I envisioned my mother's "desk" on the floor at the side of her bed.

In 1999 I had an opportunity, through Nadia and her United Nations work, to go to Kosovo. She and I had maintained an up-and-down relationship, our moments of exhilarating fun punctuated by her judgments or dismissal of me. When she became a part of Bernard Kouchner's UN cabinet in Kosovo at the end of the Serbian-Kosovar war, I pestered her to arrange entry for me into the country. I would give my photographs to the UN.

I was the voyeur-visitor, but was allowed to join two UN photographers— one Romanian, one Russian. The three of us became friends and went everywhere, often with the use of Nadia's staff car. We met early in the day and split our time between their job of photographing official moments and my own pursuit of people and their stories. I heard, through interpreters, of the horror of the war, of the betrayals of Serbian and Kosovar neighbors killing each other when just weeks before they had farmed together.

I couldn't help but feel the lure of the adrenaline and the glamour of combat, the hyped-up, we-could-die-tomorrow urgency. Despite the intensity of my several weeks' stay in Kosovo, I of course could not grasp the complicated problems

Portrait of me by my Russian colleague

that presaged the conflict, but it wasn't hard to observe war's absurd motives and rationales even while I caught glimpses of hope. I won't forget the celebration I photographed as I watched a new friendship bloom between a Serbian man and a Kosovar woman, both nationalities being inducted for the first time into the new police academy.

On a rainy afternoon I sat with a family in the remains of their house in a bombed-out village near Pristina, Kosovo's capital. The children huddled close to the mother for warmth, perhaps for protection, and paid little attention to my camera except for one staring twelve-year-old boy who had beautiful dark eyes. Outside, on a forty-foot clothesline, found clothes and objects were carefully hung for anyone looking for their loved one's belongings. My Kosovar guide Sylvia and I had brought some food and supplies, but there was little enthusiasm for this kind of help.

After we drove away, an angry and frustrated Sylvia, both hands clenching the wheel, asked me what I specifically wished to achieve by taking and showing my photographs.

"Don't you understand the country's tragedy? What are these photographs for?" she snapped. It was fair to ask. Intimidated, I answered that my intention was to show the resilient strength and the essence of the female.

"What do you mean, essence?" Again she snapped. "We are just women. We do what we are meant to do."

"But what is that?" I asked with a partial strength. "I have been photographing Kosovar women who are now in administrative positions in place of the fighting men. Will they retreat once the men return? Are your colleagues surprised by their ability to make decisions, to govern while facing war's terrors—alone with their children?"

Kosovo woman with family

Sylvia peered over at me, her short, unruly hair covering one eye.

"Yes, sometimes they are surprised by their strength."

"Where do you think that strength comes from?" I quickly went on, "I think that women have a connection to the earth, different from men, and that they are empowered by that connection. I'm not denigrating men, but women take pride in their intuitive knowledge. I hope my images reveal their wisdom." I wanted to sound sure of my conviction in talking to Sylvia, but I wasn't.

I had so many questions, I told Sylvia. I had witnessed and photographed women bonding, such as the Roma in Kosovo's gypsy camps. Their heightened sense of community seemed to be a reaction to being left out, not belonging. Overly simple as the comparison may have been, I imagined our American old-timey sewing circles, where women announced their hardships or dreams, subjects often silenced in male company.

"Do you see that in Kosovo? Women coming together like that?" I asked.

"I don't know, I don't know, what are you asking me? Do females look one another in the eye more than men do? Does it all go back to the ability to give birth? What?" Sylvia stammered, staring at me. Tears began.

"I was raped," she said suddenly.

Stunned by her candor, I whispered, "I'm so sorry." There was nothing else to say.

Of my work in Kosovo, Nadia said with sarcasm, "I see our photographers and those from other publications going one way—and yet you are always taking the opposite path, straight toward the people on the sidelines. I see you concentrating on those women. You're going for the more subtle story, I assume?" She gave me a backward glance as she walked toward the waiting journalists, their cameras poised to photograph her.

My visitor's allotted time in Kosovo ended. I took the UN bus from Pristina to the Macedonia airport, a hilariously harrowing journey, as the long lines of trucks made it nearly impossible to move forward. Impatient, after an hour of sitting and grumbling, I decided to get off the bus.

"It's only another ten miles to the airport, I'll find a car going around these trucks up ahead," I said to the young girl next to me.

She answered, "I'm coming, too."

We stepped off the bus. She put her old-fashioned wheel-less bag on top of my wheeled luggage. We pulled my two suitcases through the bellowing, smoking lines of trucks looming around us. I wish I had thought to have a picture taken of me pulling my two brand-new T. Anthony suitcases for the store's ad campaign.

The angry female customs guard at the Kosovo border tossed my passport on the ground with a curt spit of the word American. I wasn't scared. I was determined, and with that attitude, it was not difficult to maneuver my luggage over the rubble and around two dead bodies with white sheets carelessly thrown over them. Finally a ride with a French ambulance took my bus companion and me a few more miles. We finished the short journey, offering American dollars to a family whose car was so loaded down that it scraped the ground—but we made it. We arrived at the airport and found our way to separate departure gates. My plane's seating arrangement gave new meaning to the cynical, mess of war: only the last five rows in the back were for *non-smokers*. The rest of the twenty-five rows ahead were designated for smokers. I happily smoked all the way to a welcome three days alone in Rome.

Leaving Kosovo, I had a dreamy sense of freedom. Trudging through the long line of trucks belching smoke from Kosovo to the Macedonian airport had given me a clearer picture. Something had shifted in me. The familiar desire to cross into other worlds still beckoned, but had lessened. I no longer wanted to be in Nadia's tantalizing garden.

It was not that my entry into Nadia's world had been a mistake. I had simply lost myself by staying too long.

On my return to Santa Fe I sent the photographs to Nadia's staff and to UN director Kouchner.

"She has shown me something I didn't know," he told Nadia, validating my stories, the small stories I had been collecting.

Nadia and I didn't communicate much in the early years of the new millenium. We were living separate lives: she in Baghdad, again as part of the UN during the Iraqi War, I happily in Santa Fe.

One afternoon in 2003, as I stood in front of the television, I heard the news that the UN building in Baghdad—where Nadia was chief of staff in Sergio De Mello's cabinet—had been bombed. A day or two later I learned she had been killed.

I remember the far-away slow reality, the odd disconnect to my real and current life, a confusion of memories. Nadia was gone. It took a muddled period to feel my loss, that there wouldn't be any more time to ask further questions about her world, her exotic world.

She had never wanted to return to Egypt to live, unlike many in her family. But neither did she seek another country's citizenship and passport, again unlike some in her family. I had always felt she was rooted to something ancient. I assumed it to be Egypt, at least the Arab world—so perhaps it was appropriate that she died in Iraq. But in fact I don't really know to what place she belonged. That may have been part of her longing. I think back to her remark, "My people? Our future? She is behind us."

Perhaps the need to belong was something we shared, and perhaps that's what she meant that day several years after I had moved from New York and was not in a relationship. "We understand each other," she had said. "We have fun. Let's meet, I'll come to Santa Fe."

Even though I had a nightmare recently in which I was looking for Nadia's address in Cairo, telling the taxi driver it was somewhere on "Abu Ghraib Street"—the infamous place of torture—she remains a gift.

I visualize her body being wrapped in cloth—her culture's ritual—and put into the dirt of her family's square in Cairo's City of the Dead. I see a black shawl revealing the allure of black eyes.

18

Billie's Choice

Belonging is a mystery. The word infers a relationship, a membership, a sense of fitting in, and a connection that should be reliable—although the most obvious belonging, to family, is by default.

We don't choose our family; we're thrown together. Yet "Who are your people?" is a mainstay Southern question, perhaps the most important one, because if you are "family," you are a blessed soul, no matter how many transgressions you have committed—as long as you follow the Magnolia Code.

I treasured my kinship with Aunt Billie, although I saw her less and less in my older years. But in 2010 I made a visit to The Cypress, the retirement home in North Carolina where she had lived for several years. I hoped she would have answers to my questions: "What does being Southern really mean?" and Uncle Itch's tease, "Where you ever gonna belong, chile?"

My drive to The Cypress took a two-hour, back-roads sweep through the piney woods from the small town of Corwith, where Billie, neé Willa, and the rest of Mother's family had grown up. Driving down the tree-lined entrance, I saw Billie at the front door waiting for me, expectant, lofty, and looking strong, although she weighed only eighty-seven pounds. The hot time of day didn't bother Billie; she was fresh and comfortable, and her streaked grey hair, framing her vivacious face, gave her an elegance. She had a love for shoes, and that day she had on fairly high-heeled ones, with little gold buckles on the toes. Instead of the I'm-going-to-die-tomorrow-so-who-cares-that-my-slip-is-showing attitude, she clearly cared how her rust-colored, matched skirt-and-sweater set looked

Aunt Billie

with her single strand of pearls. Good looking all her life, Billie's age added to her stylish presence. She certainly wasn't a fading Southern belle; I'd always noticed that. She had her own look. I couldn't define it, but I liked it. Billie was similar to my mother in mannerisms—a certain forward stance, a slightly surprised, open expression. But they didn't look alike, and couldn't have—Billie was adopted.

I had hardly stepped out of my car when Billie hurried over, grabbed my arm, and we hugged tight. I loved the hint of her light perfume. She looked at me.

"Lord, I am thrilled to see you, just thrilled. We have so much to catch up on. Quick, let's go onto the porch. I'll smoke and you can tell me everything. We'll sit away from the other residents. Don't worry, they're happy swinging in the spring sunshine," she said, hastily greeting everyone we passed.

She sat poised, her ninety-four-year-old fingers delicately curled around a menthol cigarette. She was gently rocking, her feet lifting a few inches with every swing. Spring had come to the South early; the heavy scent of magnolia blossoms filled the air. We rolled into conversation as if it hadn't been years since my last visit. I sat across from her in an old-fashioned wicker chair. We talked of family, the people of her past, her youth.

Knowing I had driven over from her hometown, she wanted to know right away if modern times had affected Corwith.

"Is Carolina Street still the prettiest street in the world? Corwith always was a town of sweet beauty—and even sweeter secrets." Billie laughed. She had left Corwith in her twenties and didn't want to go back, not even in her old age. She had moved to The Cypress to be close to her daughter.

I told her that even though the azalea shrubs hadn't quite blossomed, Carolina Street still had a grandeur and a softness. Billie loved her childhood house, set back off the sidewalk, but close enough for walkers to give you a nod toward the beauty of the day, to make you feel a part of them—even if you didn't really want to be. She recounted how she would come home to her mother's sweet iced tea and warm cheese straws made ready for her and her friends.

"My handsome older cousin Franklin, so cute in his little bow tie, always wanted to make a visit for a time." She described the hot, steamy afternoons, everything moving slowly, and how she and Franklin couldn't wait to go to the back of the house—the "dance room," they called it— and try the new swing steps to records played on a Victrola.

"We wound that thing up tight so the song wouldn't stop in the middle of our dance," she mused dreamily. Billie said that Franklin always wanted to slow-dance.

"Sometimes ... we'd kiss. And why not? Nothin' wrong with that. Anyway, we were just playing. We'd get in the back seat of Franklin's daddy's car and smoke. When we saw someone coming down the street, we'd hide way down in that big ol' yellow Packard, couldn't stop giggling. Or we'd be daring and smoke in the house, always on the screened-in porch that looked onto the garden. I liked to watch the smoke curls go through the screen. I guess that's when I started smoking, and here I am in my nineties, still puffin' away."

Billie talked about Ben Jones, too. He was the chauffeur.

"Mother said he was like family, in everything but color." She confided that she wished she could dance with Ben, he was so good looking. "But I wasn't that crazy. Anyway, Ben wouldn't have wanted to. Lord, if we'd been caught, we'd have been killed; well ... Ben would have been killed."

It seemed like Billie's behavior was just that of a mischievous child, maybe similar to mine—not "wild" like they had always said she had acted—but at that time, maybe any deviation from the Southern belle concept was considered wild. Her curiosity and restlessness made her want to do things outside her proper world, like dancing with Ben. Maybe the appeal was in the risk, or maybe she wanted to see his black hand next to her lighter one.

I recalled a night of my own dancing, with a man from Pakistan, when I was a student in Italy. He had picked me up at the Marchesa Patrizi's house. When I returned that night, the marchesa stood waiting for me. She sternly told me to never bring an Arab into her house again. I'd been raised by parents who were prejudiced against black people, but not against Arabs. It may seem naïve, but it was only then that I realized prejudice is arbitrary. I continued to meet Hussein down the street at a café, where we would go dancing. I did like seeing his dark hand alongside mine.

Being with Billie reminded me of the story Mother had told us several times about the day Billie showed up, one late afternoon in perhaps 1919. I remember how Mother relived the story, really telling it more for herself than for us. The children were told to come quick and see the new precious child. A white blanket with an appliquéed rose design on it covered the baby. Mother had a vivid memory of that rose. She would recount how she, her brother and her mother sat on the veranda swing rocking themselves and the child, she and her brother waiting for an explanation. But there wasn't much to tell about this baby except that she had been abandoned and needed a home.

"What would you think if this lovely baby girl joined our family?" their mother asked.

The way Mother told it, she emphatically answered that this child wasn't lovely at all, that she didn't look like any of them—that dark hair, all curly like that. She wouldn't fit in. Mother didn't like her and never would.

Mother had a sad face as she recalled that moment. Her adored father had died the previous year, and her mother had soon remarried. Now she was being asked to welcome a new baby whom she feared would capture her mother's affection. She could feel the terror of that possibility.

The children were told to hush up with their complaints and bring out their Christian love. The baby was staying. That was that. And before the end of the day they were also asked to make up a birth date for little Willa Pearl—the name they had given her, which combined my grandmother's name, Pearl, with that of her brother, William, who had just died.

"Birth date? Just give her any date," they answered.

"No, that won't do for this sweet child," she said, cuddling the baby. "Wouldn't it be nice, Alice dear, to share your birthday with Willa? June is such a pretty month."

That was the end of the oft-told story. Then Mother would turn to Alicia and me, her hands clenched stiffly at her side, and say, "From then on, I hated that baby. She took my birthday away." We understood.

A woman came hobbling over to us on the porch. She appeared somewhat baffled, but her presence was lively. She wore a perfectly ironed flowery dress, her cane sporting an enthusiastic plastic spray of flowers twined around it. Most of the others, shuffling behind walkers, looked lost and, as Billie said, paid no mind to their appearance.

Billie got up and helped Betty Ann find a chair in the sun, making sure the sweet but addled lady wasn't sitting too near us. She came back and told me that Betty Ann had become so mixed up lately that one night, when she had gone across the hall to Betty Ann's apartment to take her out to supper, she had told Billie to go downstairs and "tell my parents that I'm coming, I'll be right down."

Billie said she became impatient and told her, "Betty Ann, your parents are not downstairs, they are in heaven, and you're going to see them soon enough. Now let's go."

As she talked to Betty Ann, I pulled out my small camera to sneak photographs of Billie. Her facial expressions always showed a touch of joy. But when she sat back down in her rocker, a frown appeared. She didn't explain, but straightened her sleeves and pulled out her compact to perform the powdering-of-one's-nose routine, allowing the gestures to slowly free her from uncomfortable memories that were crowding in. I knew she didn't want to get stuck in a mood; she wanted to have fun. Billie and fun went together. She saw life with an amused eye.

She then suggested that it might be time to go down to the corner café and have some truth and "memory juice."

"You know, a nice little glass of white wine. It's just a tacky café, but it'll do. I like it. They say memory has its own truth, you know that, don't you, Joanie?

Come on. I'd sneak a drink out on this porch, but then all those people on walkers would come over for a nip."

We settled into a booth at Geraldine's Café, just down the street from The Cypress. It was a Friday afternoon, so the locals—some in ties or work shirts, all looking for an early start to the weekend—were filtering in. Many greeted Billie; she was one of the café characters, I surmised. I asked how often she went there. She told me just one or two times a week. I bet not, I said to myself. Bet she's a regular.

Billie ordered her wine. She didn't care what the label was, just so it was white. She flirted with the waiters, knew their names, even let one of them give her hand a kiss. That pleased her. Brought up with Southern charm, she knew how to use it and have fun with it, make it work for her.

Jazz played on the local radio station. Someone yelled, "Turn it up, that's smooth."

Billie stared at a dancing couple, shy to begin their swings into the rhythmic step of *Stormy Weather*. Billie loved that song—it made her think of good times, especially with her darling second husband, Francis. She told me she loved everything about Francis, including his yachts.

I pretended I was shocked.

"His yachts?" I repeated. "You didn't marry him for his money, by any chance, did you?"

"Well, of course! But I did love him. I had to survive. How was a woman with two children, one drunk ex-husband and no money going to make it? The one job I could find was selling jewelry at some half-baked store. Well, that and two nickels was going to get me a bus ride, nothin' more than that. I made Francis laugh. I took care of him. He took care of me. We had a good time. Why shouldn't I marry him? Your mother didn't approve, I knew that. But I certainly couldn't go to her for help. So, I ask you, who was going to help me?" She lit another cigarette with a flip of her gold Dupont lighter, the one with Francis' initials on it.

Simple as that, I thought.

Billie ordered another glass of wine, said she didn't care that she wasn't supposed to have more than one. At ninety-four, what did it matter? I too had a second glass. She wanted to talk about my mother, "Sis," she called her. She said they had different versions of the adoption story.

"Do you know what I was told? That some lovely person on a beautiful spring day had left me in a basket on my new mother's porch. Can you believe that? Hell, I'm not a complete idiot. I mean are we supposed to break out in song with that hogwash? Hogwash truth, I call it. Someone must have known where I came from."

"Yes, somebody must have," I agreed. But I felt impatience as I remembered Mother's side of the story. "That wasn't right, that Mother was asked to share her birthday with you. That was insensitive. It was her special day."

"Yes, I suppose so," she said, "How could Mother do that to Sis? Sis must have hated me."

That was all Billie said for a while.

"Billie, I often think about your cat, Bastet. Did she really protect you? You told me she gave you courage."

"Hell, yes, my Bastet, and Lord could she whirl, twirled all the opposites right into her tail. Yes'm, her balance was in her tail, like for most cats. That's how I saw it. I loved Bastet; she helped me in my times of trouble. One particular time she surely did. I'll tell you about that some day."

Billie fell silent as she stared off at a clock on the wall that had a string of plastic daisies around it. It was five p.m. The music started up again. A 1930s mellow jazz piece, *The Way You Look Tonight*, began. More people crowded the tiny dance floor. Lights were lowered, chairs were pushed to the side, scraping the floor; a muffled laugh came from the next booth.

"I do so love to dance," she murmured. Wine had seeped into Billie's emotions. She laid her head back on the red vinyl booth seat.

"I think Sis knew who my real parents were, maybe everyone knew. Damn the secrets."

I held my breath and waited.

"I may have figured out who my father was, Joanie."

"My cousin told me that William, Mother's younger brother, had gotten some girl pregnant, and the family felt obligated to adopt the baby—*bet it was me*," Billie exclaimed in a louder tone.

"It was the Christian thing to do," Mother would have said. Billie was satisfied with that thought because if her uncle actually was her father, then she wasn't some sort of stray. She was family.

"Why hadn't anyone told me? That's what upset me, not telling me that I might really be family. That's what sent me to the Gypsy," Billie said.

"That's when I got my cat, Bastet."

I nodded my understanding. It all made sense.

We sat quietly for a while.

I had been looking at Billie while listening to her imaginings. And I saw something that I hadn't seen before, when she was younger. A new feature stood out in her lovely face, perhaps more so now in her aging face.

I suddenly wondered if she had black blood in her background.

With the help of the wine and the dreamy strains of music, I opened myself to my own imaginings as Billie recalled a story about Ben, her family's chauffeur.

"You remember me telling you about Ben, don't you, Joanie?"

"Yes, I do, you liked him a lot."

"He came to see me many years ago, before I moved north, to deliver a message from a woman named Sarah Langdon, who had occasionally worked as a seamstress for my family. He told me how pretty she was, that she sang in his church choir and could do fine things with a needle.

"Then he added, 'But now she's dying and wants to see people from her past. She said she loved your family and remembered a precious little baby girl whose name was Willa. Sarah asked me if I knew where you were, would I ask you to visit. I told her I could find you, you were just a town away.'

"But I didn't remember this woman, Joanie." I asked Ben, 'What does this have to do with me?' "

Billie was silent for a moment, gazing wistfully at the dancers.

"I was thinking of Ben the other day and his strange story, how much I liked him, and I recalled that woman's odd request. I guess in my old age, Joanie, I'm remembering all sorts of things. Maybe she and Mother had some sort of bond. Ben liked her, he said that."

"And what happened, Aunt Billie?" I asked. "Did you visit her?"

"No. No, I didn't. And she died a few days later. I felt bad, but I just couldn't make a deathbed visit to someone I didn't even know.

"Well, maybe I should have," she added.

"Oh, for pity's sake, let's go on back to The Cypress, Joanie, I'm plumb worn out. Maybe we'll find another memory—something a little lighter." She laughed.

We drove back to The Cypress and made our way to the veranda.

"We'll sit a spell," Billie said. "We need a breeze."

I too was tired. Billie's tale was so complicated. I closed my eyes and let my mind wander back over the conversation. I began to create a scenario that could meet the adoption mystery. I wanted to ask Billie, "Do you think Ben was suggesting that you and Sarah were more closely connected somehow?" But I knew it was best not to ask. *Just leave it*, I said to myself. If they were more closely connected, then Billie had made a choice, a difficult, deeply complicated choice.

The tears now pooling in my eyes weren't for Sarah or for Billie. They were for the irony of the story, this very Southern story. Billie's possible father would have made her a true family member. But her possible mother would have made her an outcast.

I remembered Billie's warning to me long ago.

"There are always choices and consequences, that's for goddamn sure, Joanie. But don't look back. You can't change anything. And anyway, as long as nothing is said out loud—well, that's how we are down here in Dixie," Billie said in a sing-song voice. "Cover up, hush up, best not to talk about it. Yes'm, like they say, 'It's all moonlight and magnolias.' I'm damn sure about that."

It had grown cool in the late afternoon; shawls were laid out for the residents. Billie wrapped herself in a plaid one and put her head back on the cushioned rocking chair. Her eyes closed, she began to softly hum.

Night and day, you are the one ... only you....

I watched Billie rock and hum herself into a dreamy place. I heard her whisper to her memories, "Franklin, let's dance to this one. Turn up the volume, just a bit. Yes, go wind up that Victrola again. Oh, that's smooth."

19

The Burial

"I want you girls to dig up your father."

My mother's eighty-nine-year-old voice came through my mobile phone quietly and distinctly, her accent as strong as ever. She made the request without as much as a hello.

Staying at Nadia's apartment in New York for a meeting with my New York gallery, I had groggily answered the very early morning call. I stared at the phone, hoping to concentrate. My father had died several years before.

My parents had argued about their burial sites forever. The subject, usually brought up at the dinner table, was a reliable source of irritation for both of them.

Out of nowhere Mother would start.

"I don't want to be with your family."

My father retorted with bluster.

"What's wrong with my family?"

His answer was a charged cue for one of the responses kept in my mother's semi-locked-but-ready-to-explode mental vault.

"They're a clique! They leave me out and don't make me feel good. They're always laughing and making fun. No, I want to be buried with my family, in my hometown. And you should be with me. Besides, North Carolina is more beautiful than Florida."

"Oh, Alice," Father answered. "My family loves you, you just don't see it. But," he added casually, "maybe it's best for you to go to your family and I to mine."

I saw Mother look down at her plate and move the vegetables and half-eaten roasted lamb from side to side. She did that often. We waited.

"But we're a family. Don't you want to be with me?"

"Oh, for heaven's sake, of course I do. Don't be silly."

Once the burial conversation had started, there was little chance for diversion, or for parental attention to come our way. All three sisters—Barrett, Alicia, and I—would look from one parent to the other with apprehension as their angry voices rose. After years of the same old argument, we gave our attention to fiddling with our food or whispering, covertly watching to see if Mother would soon push the kitchen buzzer that lay somewhere beneath the rug under the table. The sound alerted Sophie to come in with dessert. This at least would cause a distraction, if not a full-on rescue, for us. Finally the fragrance of the crusty cherry pie, the one Mother had purchased that afternoon at the German bakery, drifted around the swinging door.

My parents sat at opposite ends of the table; the chasm between them seemed to lengthen as dinner went on. They were dressed for dinner, Father always in a jacket and tie and Mother in a dress, stepped up from her daytime wear. Alicia and I squirmed in matching outfits, our white dresses with the green vine growing up the side. Alicia didn't like the twin look at all. Barrett sat correctly in her favorite brown skirt and sweater, which set off her red hair. She wore suede high heels recently bought for the coming Christmas parties. Taking it upon herself to be grown-up, in that older sister manner, she tried to start a conversation.

"At school, we've been learning about a man called Darwin."

"Who's Darwin?" Alicia asked.

"He's an important figure in history," Mother interrupted. "We'll look him up later in the encyclopedia. For now, you girls eat your dinner."

"But I want to tell you what I learned," Barrett said, bravely ignoring her dismissal.

"Yes, yes, and we want to know, but your father and I are having a serious conversation."

Alicia started fiddling with her knife and fork.

"Put those down, Alicia. You leave utensils on the table."

We stared at our plates or looked toward the side window at the thick damask curtains where green birds perched on brown branches. I squinted at the birds, willing them to come alive. I charged the leaves to turn and rustle. But nothing happened. On the sideboard, placed correctly and polished to a shine, were silver candlesticks, bowls, and animal figures, adding to the room's formality. Little shell ashtrays awaited Father's after-dinner cigarettes, the object of my focus as the smoke rose and curled.

"Daddy, make smoke rings."

Obliging us, his mouth formed a perfect "O," just like the Camel cigarette man on the Times Square billboard.

Sometimes frustrated, in the middle of the going-nowhere burial conversation, Mother would return to the topic of school.

"John. Ask them about school. You never ask the girls any questions. Just ask them something, John."

He glared, irritated at her, across the table. He put down his fork, took a gulp of the scotch and soda that sat in front of him.

"Joanie, when was the war of 1812?"

We looked at him and then at Mother's flushed and frustrated face. We knew we shouldn't laugh, but how could we help it? Father was funny.

Amused at his joke, Father leaned back in his chair.

"Anyway, I'm not sure North Carolina is so much prettier than Florida. What do you girls think?"

Nothing was ever resolved regarding the location of burial sites. My father died first. His body went to his birthplace in Jacksonville, Florida, to lie next to his family. Mother's health declined after that, but no longer did she speak of the burial issue. Still, the subject obviously had been churning in her head.

"Dig up Daddy, is that what you said?" I asked, astonished.

"Yes, I've made a decision. I'm not long for this world. Your father and I always had such a happy time. We should be together. I want you to send his body to Corwith. We'll continue to be happy in my hometown."

Three daughters

Even though my eyes rolled at her fantasy of their "happy time," I appreciated the need to cling to a positive memory. And why not? In fact, there had been happy times.

I answered in as sweet a voice as I could muster, searching for the old images.

"Yes, I remember. I remember the two of you dancing."

"Oh, we certainly did love to dance." Her voice trailed off.

I could see them, Father holding her tight, moving them slowly around the living room. They were good dancers. They held on, oblivious to us and to their previous mean words.

I didn't know how to continue the discussion on the phone and besides, I needed to leave for my meeting. I could barely see out of the dark apartment window, but I heard a smattering of rain. The subway would be crowded. I might have just enough time to wash my hair, then dry it under the subway ceiling fan.

Impatiently, I said, "Well, I'll discuss this with Alicia and Barrett to see if this is even possible. We'll have to call Uncle Jimmie. You know he might say Father belongs with his family, too."

"Okay, call Jimmie and let me know. But remember, I'm your father's wife; Jimmie's just his brother."

I hung up and looked out the rain-streaked window, envisioning a dreary black-and-white scene of shovels and pitchforks lifting the dirt from Father's grave.

The urgent calls to my sisters would have to wait until a break in my meeting.

At noon I phoned, relieved they were available, doing wifely things in their apartments. Each responded to my explanation with a short silence, followed by giggles.

"Dig Daddy up?" Alicia asked, and Barrett, who loved the word "absurd," yelled it into her phone.

In the early evening we met at Barrett's home and sat on the floor with glasses of wine. Compassion, anger, then impatience overtook us. The expression, "Oh, for God's sake" ended in, "All right, let's call Uncle Jimmie, but Joanie, you call him, Mother spoke to you first."

Annoyed at my burden, I argued, "Why can't she call him? It's her idea."

Alicia answered in a soft voice.

"She's just not capable. Uncle Jimmie has always scared her. They all scare her. It's as if they're jumping out of the closet at her."

"Okay, I'll call, but he'll have a fit, you know that. Like Aunt Miggie once said in that funny deep drawl of hers, 'My brother Jimmie is a noisy, powerful man with whom nobody argues.'

"And—just by the way—do you know what a racist he is? Did you ever hear him?" I asked Alicia and Barrett. They looked at me, waiting.

"I did, one day sitting by his pool in Jacksonville; horrible, mean as a snake, those remarks."

"Well, forget all that. Try to remember a good side before you call him," Barrett said in her steady voice.

"Anyway," I added, "how can he be mad at me? I'm just the messenger; it's Mother who's making the request."

"True. Good luck," they sarcastically chimed in.

After visiting galleries, I went home and paced the apartment's small living room, taking time out to spy across the side street with Nadia's binoculars, still one of my favorite pastimes. I wished Nadia had been in New York so I could hear her sardonic view on the predicament, but she was in Europe for the United Nations.

Another memory of Uncle Jimmie bubbled up. Late one afternoon in New York, he and his intimidating, glamorous wife, Lina— short for Carolina—came to visit. I was probably five. I sat in the guest room with them while they had a drink. They began to argue. As their voices rose, I froze in my chair, staring at them, scared.

"Quiet, Lina, keep your voice down," he demanded.

She became angry and turned her impatience toward me.

"And why are you still here?"

I started crying, and as I began to run out of the room, I heard my uncle say, "Why take your anger out on that sweet child? It's me you're mad at. And you better quit being mad."

The memory of Uncle Jimmie sticking up for me, plus my drained glass of wine, gave me confidence.

"Uncle Jimmie, hello."

We went on with family pleasantries until I interrupted nervously.

"I have a request from our mother." I began to explain.

He broke into our conversation.

"Well ... if that would make her happy," he said with a hint of impatience.

Bewildered, I stammered, "Uncle Jimmie, I thought—"

"You know, Joanie, marriage and family, it's just a strange combination. Lord only knows what goes on, and I'm not entirely sure the Lord himself does know. I loved my brother—more than I can say, I loved him. But I could see your mother often suffered. She felt left out. He made fun of her when he shouldn't have. In front of us. That wasn't right."

"You saw that, Uncle Jimmie?"

"Oh, yes, I did, and I was sorry he did that. So, Joanie, if that's what your mother wants, it's okay with me."

Barrett, Alicia and I met again and I repeated Uncle Jimmie's words: "If that's what your mother wants."

"Wants?" We repeated. What had she wanted, really wanted, all those years, from Father? We each answered with our own version: love, protection, attention for a lovely but shy Southern girl, support in her many moments of insecurity and, certainly, to shine as Father's only one—which she wasn't. Now she could have him with her for keeps, buried deep in the earth next to her, and in her hometown—far away from the Baker clan.

"Will their fighting finally stop?" Alicia asked with irony in her voice.

"He never wanted to go to Corwith, he made his choice long ago," Barrett said. "Why change now? To move him seems like defying the gods."

We looked at the situation from all sides. Our decision was unanimous. Father would stay put in his original grave.

But it didn't end there. We thought of a way they could be together but separate— as they had been in life.

It hadn't come easily, this solution.

"I'm not sure, will the church consider this as interference or something like that?" Alicia asked.

With our decision sitting on fairly solid ground, I called Mother the next day.

"We have an answer."

I spoke in a quiet tone, concerned not to rattle her.

"When you die, you will be cremated. Then we'll divide your ashes between yours and Daddy's burial sites. We'll have two separate funerals. Celebrate your life twice. But your ashes will be together."

Silence. I waited, gripping the receiver, wondering if I was ready for a negative answer.

"Are you there?" I asked.

"Yes, I'm here," she answered in a surprisingly sprightly tone. "That would be fine. In fact, Joanie, that would be very nice."

In disbelief, my hand reached for my forehead.

"Really? What do you mean? Are you saying yes?"

"Yes, you girls have come up with a very reasonable solution. I can cope with the Baker clan for half the year. And that's how I wish to see it." Perhaps Mother's idea of "half the year" was a fantasy, but it made sense to her.

She died near Christmas. As she had requested, the two burials waited until spring, "When the weather and flowers, especially the magnolias, are at their Southern best."

20

The Black Madonna

As a ritual, my father taught me to say "rabbit, rabbit, rabbit" for good luck on the first day of each new month. I was about eight, just old enough to be respectful of such precise directions.

"Say the three words after midnight, but before conversing with anyone. Remember, you're not to speak to any soul until you say the three words."

Also, on the morning of the month's first day—if we were at our summer home in the mountains—Father and I would descend from the second-floor bedrooms walking backwards down the stairs—in order to avoid confronting the dark spirit head on, he warned. Despite his laugh, I knew deep down he truly believed the superstition.

I no longer live in a house with stairs, so that ritual has been scratched, but I dreamily call out "rabbit, rabbit, rabbit" between midnight and morning on the first day of the month, just in case.

While Father had many superstitions, I have only a few. I do practice rituals, keep talismans, and feel comforted by my concept of a spiritual connection "out there." I have no idea what awaits me after death, but no one has convinced me that there is nothing in the Great Beyond. I am not particularly looking for confirmation either way—just comfort.

In my childhood no one spoke about religion in a convincing or loving manner. My parents and Nanny and Sophie told me Bible stories that seemed nice and mysterious, but not real, just fanciful. I was raised Presbyterian, and from age six on I went to Sunday school at the Brick Church, up the street from

The Black Madonna and the Dancer   Monotype

our apartment. I liked to memorize the Psalms and to receive a new Bible as a reward, but in truth I often skipped Sunday school. I may have told my parents that I would walk the two blocks to the church (while they went to a midtown church), but instead I found my friend Chrissie and we bought Popsicles with some of the thirty-five cents meant for the collection plate. We liked to explore, and one Sunday morning Chrissie and I found and climbed the stairs to the roof of the building connected to the sanctuary. The teacher, who panicked and came to retrieve us, told us that the congregation had gasped at the sight of two little girl angels floating past the sanctuary's windows.

My reverence did not increase during my boarding school days. On Sundays, I sat in the pew, my short-veiled little hat perched on my head, trying to listen, but instead giggling with my friends. As usual, we were told to be quiet, to behave. But I couldn't. My rebellious spirit kept me in trouble those years at Miss Hall's School; I was constantly grounded, so I rarely ventured beyond the campus boundaries. Still, for three years the school provided a sense of safety I hadn't known.

One teacher—Miss Witherspoon, a Southerner who reminded me of my mother— tried to understand me. She would always end our conversations about my mischievous behavior on a positive note.

"You're going to grow into a fine young woman," she would say. "But, Joanie, you'd better be careful. Your wild spirit could get you in trouble." But my spirit wasn't wild—just alive.

The experiences I had known in my Protestant world didn't offer the *magic* of Catholicism. To me, their rituals were simply superstitions in another form. Eating the body of Christ was alarming.

"What does that mean?" I asked Nanny about communion one day. "What is everyone doing?" I'm sure she answered, but I don't remember.

I liked the informality of being allowed to wander in and out of St. Patrick's Cathedral on Fifth Avenue. I lit candles and thrilled to the dizziness I felt from the cloying incense fragrance as I stared at the parade of priests wearing lavish and colored robes, sprinkling holy water on the congregation.

In my twenties, I became a semi-enthusiastic member of the Fifth Avenue Presbyterian Church, where my parents were members. I enjoyed the singing and belonging to a community. I stared at the diverse group, and appreciated the church's dare in the late sixties of having Duke Ellington and Lena Horne perform for a packed uptown crowd. But I never felt involved; I just attended.

As a young woman spending time in Europe, I began to feel the oppressiveness of the Catholic Church. When I climbed the steps to the grand entrances of the cathedrals, I was forced to lift my head and look up—to the sacred, the lofty, and for me, the unattainable. I didn't know much about the Virgin Mary except that she was a symbol of purity, but why? Why did she own such a high level of goodness? I was an ordinary yet soul-seeking human being; her perfection made her seem unreachable.

I asked the obvious questions. Why did she have to be a virgin? Why were the nuns always dressed in drab gray when the priests wore colors? Why were the cathedrals so rich and adorned, yet full of poor people?

When I lived in Estaca I often visited Christ in the Desert Monastery, about an hour and a half drive north of Santa Fe, the last half-hour on a washboard dirt road along the slow-moving and lovely Chama River. The monastery's stark beauty and silence in the middle of the New Mexican desert was captivating.

The chapel, a short walk from the guest's simple cells—each containing a slim bed, a desk that looked out into the trees, and a corner kiva fireplace—provided an undisturbed world. And the monastery's eight services a day had a serenity, especially if I managed to blank out most of the monk's patriarchal comments, which usually referred to women as those who serve, or sinners with regard to their bodies. For a woman to claim her own authority was not a serious subject in this holy place.

One early morning service I heard the usual invitation to take communion, to be part of the monk's community. Despite the fact that I was not a Catholic, I was invited to participate and often did. But that morning I had concentrated on the words of the chants, and for the first time truly heard the emphasis on the male. An insensitivity pervaded the atmosphere. A quote from St. Paul, "Adam was not deceived, but the woman being deceived was in the transgression" stopped me. Woman, the sole sinner? No fault assigned to the man? I finally grasped the stunning words—and I didn't leave the pew. Why would I want to be part of a community that thinks I am inferior? I felt justified staying seated on my beautifully handcarved wooden bench.

The wind had been fierce during the service. Halfway through the homily, the door to the chapel suddenly flew open and a black cat ran in, almost leaping through the front entrance, racing toward and around the lectern, then out the back. The other guests and the monks hardly took notice.

Had I imagined the cat? No, I hadn't. The spirit of Bastet, the Goddess' black cat, had appeared, I was sure. Was it an omen, a warning? I cared for the monastery and its rituals, but now I saw how out of step, out of balance, the Church had remained. Denying the positive intrinsic power of the female and placing the burden of blame on woman is an easy answer, one that loses any possibility of integration, a balance of both genders' energies. For the Catholic Church, there is no dance of union. The Church has its own set of rules, not unlike the Magnolia Code; follow the rules and you will be rewarded. But I now know the promise is a false one, in both cases.

The oppressive values clashed loudly with the gentle beauty of the place. I left and drove down the dirt road by the extraordinary river, away from the pull of the monks' uneasy serenity. I didn't run from the monastery; I didn't feel torn. But I was unsure if or when I would return.

It seems to me the real purpose of all the Church dogma about "the light" is to keep the darkness at bay. Why? I think of my background, my parents' avoidance of dark issues.

"Keep your conversation on the light side, Joanie, no need to go into or tell your troubles." My parents told me not to delve into the dark side of life, but I would learn from the Black Madonna that the darkness was precisely where the answers were hidden.

When I saw the 1993 documentary film *Latcho Drom*, a story of the Roma people, I started to understand spiritual faith from a different perspective. In the film there is a scene in the crypt of the Catholic Church of Saintes Maries de la Mer in the Camargue, Southern France. Roma men approach a life-sized statue of their patroness, the Black Madonna, known as Ste. Sara Kali. The men crowd Ste. Sara, playing their guitars, singing, coming close, touching her, whispering in her ear. They are telling her their secrets, I said to myself. I want the same connection. In that moment, something changed in me. The sensuous scene was different from the times I had witnessed worshippers with the white Virgin Mary. I wasn't familiar with the Romas' intimacy with Ste. Sara, but I felt captured. I longed to know the Black Madonna story.

About the same time I saw the film, I had a hysterectomy, resulting in a surprise diagnosis of ovarian cancer. The doctor entered my room after the surgery and told me they had found and removed the cancer.

Cancer? I was stunned, emotional, confused.

I didn't put the pieces together at the time of my operation, but now it's obvious. At forty-nine, I saw life through questioning eyes. Now I had cancer. The irony of having lost female parts to a hysterectomy pushed me to search more deeply for the core of femaleness. Fear for my future and an already deep curiosity regarding the intrinsic nature of Woman led me to recognize feminine strength and vulnerability in a new way. The film, the cancer, my curiosity— all led me on a quest to connect with the Black Madonna.

With enough money to travel and gracious invitations to show my photographic results in Santa Fe and New York, I started down an uncharted path to discover the symbol of the Black Virgin and her differences from the Virgin Mary.

In hand was Ean Begg's book, *The Cult of the Black Virgin*, which goes into detail about hidden shrines and extraordinary displays honoring the icon. There are more than 400 Black Madonna sites in France and Italy alone.

My first and most memorable visit to a site began with my friend, Kay, another Black Madonna devotee. We climbed the many steps to the immense abbey in Einsiedeln, Switzerland, and right away came upon the Black Madonna's presence in the Lady Chapel. She filled the black marble space in front of eight or so rows of chairs. Touches of the color pink could be seen throughout the church. Known as "the best-dressed Madonna in the world," her very black figure was adorned magnificently. The monks liked to change her clothes, sometimes bundling her in several layers. I watched the monks' overt admiration as they sang to her, a ritual they performed every day. It was an experience almost as personal as the Roma scene in *Latcho Drom*.

I learned that the cult of the Black Madonna is a product of the ninth to twelfth centuries when many statues—mostly small, mostly wooden—were brought to Europe from the Holy Land by the returning crusaders. Many scholars believe her cult arose from that of the ancient Egyptian goddess, Isis.

Her blackness is controversial. I spoke to many priests about it.

"She is black from the candle smoke," several said. This made no sense to me; if smoke blackens a statue, then why are there so many white Virgin Marys in incense-filled churches? And I had taken opportunities to look under a few lavish outfits; I saw that the Madonnas' entire bodies were black, not just their exposed hands and feet.

"She is painted black to resemble the indigenous people," another priest said. But two of the most famous Black Madonnas are in Poland and Switzerland, hardly countries known for dark-skinned cultures. Several times the priests told me in a harsh tone, "There is no Black Madonna here." Or they dismissed her importance and told me to look for her "somewhere in the back of the church."

But there were other priests who had positive answers and helped expand my knowledge of her history and meaning.

For those who see her as a powerful symbol, her blackness represents the earth and therefore fertility, rebirth, creation. Her blackness is synonymous with wisdom. I was told that to access that wisdom, those of us who dare must venture into the dark and mysterious waters within, for only in that womblike place can we truly find ourselves. That is the promise of the Black Madonna: that we will find an opening into the light of self-knowledge.

The Swiss psychiatrist Carl Jung saw the Black Madonna's transformative powers—the eternal power of the feminine—as a symbol of renewal of the life force. But the ultimate message is that one has to nourish one's own seed— the power is within.

The Black Madonna   187

The Virgin Mary holds her own power, and her position as an intermediary is an important one. But she doesn't offer me what the Black Madonna does: the importance of pursuing one's own power and voice, one's own divine self-knowledge. I cheer for the wise, earthy Black Madonna who mirrors an encouraging promise back to us.

At a Black Madonna festival in South America, my friend China (who had written the book *Longing for Darkness*, which greatly influenced my Black Madonna quest), heard the priest admonish the exuberant singing and dancing celebrants, "Stop! Be more like Mary … be obedient, reasonable, serene. Above all obedient!"

China went to the priest and asked him whether anyone praises Mary for her dark side.

"It exists," she said. "Mary, as the Black Madonna, the Dark One, the other side of the Virgin Mary, she is not so obedient; she carries an earthy, fierce energy."

"The dark side?" the priest answered. "The Church is the bulwark against the dark. Come to us, it is here you will find your guidance. We offer you the light. You cannot do it alone."

"But the church doesn't look at its own darkness." China argued. "Why?" she asked.

The priest had little to say.

At Easter in 2002 I was alone in an ugly, crowded and over-lit church in Foggia in Southern Italy. I watched worshippers climb the narrow steps to the niche containing the five-foot image of a Black Madonna named Maria Santissima Incoronata. The onlookers remained fixated for a long moment before they descended. I was overwhelmed, tears ran down my face. I knew I had to find out why I was so moved. After the service—repeated every hour on such a holy day—I spoke in my faltering Italian to the people gathered outside as they celebrated, playing cards, eating, and dancing. They let me photograph their picnics while they explained their ideas about the differences between the black icon and the Virgin Mary.

"She is one of us," one woman answered simply. "She is not too good, not so high up there," she laughed, pointing to the heavens.

"We like her. She believes in us. She accepts us—the good and the bad," a round and jovial woman added. "She reminds us of ourselves."

I found a room in a seaside hotel twenty minutes from Foggia. I walked into a large bedroom with a lone bed and a side table. Hanging over the bed was a crudely-framed image of the beloved Incoronata, giving the loneliness of the room and the damp sea air a slight warmth. I took photographs of her, the bed, and the solitary chair on the balcony looking out to sea. I wondered whether the room had housed holiday vacationers or other Incoronata devotees. Were they disappointed by this dreary room, or was being with the adored Madonna enough?

I knew there were three more Black Madonnas in a village nearby. The woman behind the hotel desk said, "Oh, you will never find the tiny church by yourself. Look, over there in the café, the two motorcycle police. They'll show you."

The café beckoned with the scent of garlic, onions, and good cigarette smoke. The morning chatter and the sound of the espresso machine lever being pulled filled the air. I went over to the policemen to tell them of my plight.

"Sí, Signora, nearby, they are our very own Black Madonnas. Follow us."

The ride behind the two police on their fancy motorcycles, honking their way through the village to the dead-end dirt road location of the church, gave me a thrill. The policemen looked back and laughed at my mimicking of queen-like waves out the window to the questioning villagers standing on narrow streets in front of family stores. The people waved back.

"We love the Madonna; she loves us," the policemen said. This ride alone was worth it all, a simple tribute from me to the Madonna. I had found ordinary people who legitimized her humanness, and I was temporarily invited into their world of adoration. I love my own people, but Italians are sensuous, more informal—just like their food. They seem to laugh at themselves a lot. Not that Americans are dour, we enjoy a good time. In fact, a Frenchman once

Yemayá, Goddess of the Sea

commented that if he walked into a dining room full of every nationality, and one table was laughing, it would be the American table. I liked that thought. I don't want to be Italian, or Indian, or anything other than American, even though I do want to enter other worlds.

I had a similar reaction to a Black Madonna in Cuba. On a side street in Trinidad, through a half-opened door, I saw a small black doll representing Yemayá, goddess of the sea and of the fish. I can still envision her so clearly, sitting in an unpretentious doll-sized chair in the middle of the room, a white turban and a long white dress covering her. Light from a window streamed inside, illuminating her body and shining on the fish painted on the sea-blue walls. A long, narrow shadow stretched from her figure across the room. The scene had a gentle power, in part because of its simplicity, quietly integrating both her light and the darkness of her shadow. Yemayá's presence filled the room without demand for adulation or a lofty placement, making our necks strain upwards in reverence. To be on the same level with the Great Mother in this room required sitting on the floor. Like other Black Madonnas I had seen, Yemayá embodied the belief that we already carry the power we need inside ourselves, and that we belong to ourselves. As the worshipper at the picnic said, "She is one of us."

Ste. Sara Kali

Every May 24 and 25, the Roma gather in Saintes Maries de la Mer to worship their Ste. Sara Kali. It is a time of celebration and reunion. Adoring the Madonna, they ask for her protection for the independent lives they dare to live, and for the healing of their misfortunes. They allowed me to mingle with them. Their white vans were circled in an intimate communion. I photographed the twirling dances of the sensuous rhythms of the Roma music, skirts flying, bracelets jangling, an evocative splendor of colors. I wanted to jump in, to have that same feeling.

The dance is part of the atmosphere of passion, an unselfconscious, slightly frenzied time, culminating in the afternoon Mass. The day was hot. We crowded into the church, waiting for the statue of Ste. Sara to be brought up from the crypt. In the anticipatory fervor, I felt moments of anxiety and looked around for a possible exit. No one sat. We all stood with expectation.

Once Ste. Sara emerged, the chanting began. Eventually the crowd left the church to start the procession of the priests, the Roma, and the onlookers thronging the narrow streets. Some rode white Camargue horses, holding Ste. Sara on high until they entered the sea to wash her body. I followed, welcoming the cool water around my legs as I waded in a T-shirt, white pants, and sturdy sandals. We stood in the surf up to our knees, and, mesmerized, I joined in the calling for Sara Kali. This was not just religious ritual; it was belief made concrete, a moment of connection to the intense, if ephemeral, feeling of possibility and hope. They were handling her body, her veils were trailing off atop the water, and part of her lay exposed. No action was rude—maybe passionate and personal—but not rude. I felt dizzy.

In the early 2000s Kay and I met up again at the Chartres Cathedral, an hour west of Paris. Both of us wanted to see the two Chartres Black Madonnas—Notre Dame de Pilar and the Madonna Sous Terre—and also to walk the cathedral's magnificent thirteenth-century labyrinth. I learned that labyrinths were originally created as early as 1800 B.C. in Egypt. All labyrinths represent a pilgrimage, a spiritual journey. It is appropriate that the Cathedral houses the labyrinth and the Black Madonna, as the intimacy in walking the labyrinth's path echoes the intimacy found in the Black Madonna's path to self-knowledge.

Thirty of us gathered for the weeklong study of the labyrinth in Chartres, each for various reasons. At the end of the week's intense studies we all walked the last evening's joyful yet solemn path, lit by thousands of votives, accompanied by an *a cappella* choir through the corridors of the crypt up to the nave of the church. The cathedral is enormous—able to hold at least 10,000—but the labyrinth feels safe and contained.

I had walked the labyrinth many times, and found it easy to feel and respect the power of the path. But that night I was anxious. I had told my spiritual guide that I was troubled I wouldn't "get it," that I wouldn't find my own meaning of the labyrinth, that I had been skimming the surface of the deep experience. We began the evening sitting silently in the crypt, where we were asked to write a word or phrase on a piece of paper regarding a question or answer we needed defined. I had written the word "access." We put our papers in a stone bowl in front of the Madonna Sous Terre.

In the nave, a hush enveloped us as we waited our turn to begin. Each was allowed distance from other walkers. I started my slow pace in the aura of the candlelight across the labyrinth's forty-foot expanse.

I felt alone, even in the midst of other walkers—the same aloneness I had felt in the Black Madonna crowds—alone while among so many. The damp of the church quickened my step, and I swung my arms, wishing I had warmer clothes. I heard coughs in the distance, but the overpowering, almost wailing pitch of the singing canceled any intrusive sounds and gave me a dreamy sense of floating: down one side of the labyrinth, across, skip a line, look at the pattern, reach the center where even nonbelievers feel the rising energy. Some turned and turned as they walked. I thought of the Roma who would have danced their way to the labyrinth's center of power. I wished the light from the exquisite stained-glass rose windows would last, but the darkness was fast falling on the entire church.

A quote by Edward C. Whitmont filtered into my mind.

"One of the oldest images of the mystery of life, death, transformations, and return is the labyrinth in which we fear to lose ourselves."

Halfway along the path, I felt the sudden strong presence of an entity next to me.

Surprised and jolted, I pulled away, but the feeling persisted.

"Who's there?" I asked silently.

"Your mother," came her quiet answer.

Completely confused, I kept walking, hoping silence would return. My mother had died in 2001. This was a year later. How could she be here? Please go away, I begged to say out loud. In a bewildered state, I looked at my feet, and concentrated on the scent of the votives, the distant sound of the chanting. Along with my disbelief in her presence, I guarded myself against the voice of the person who would mock my intention.

"Joanie," I could hear her say, "why are you so serious? Stop asking so many questions. That's just not worth anything."

My mother's own lack of self-confidence had always overridden my needs and longings. She scared me, especially when I was young and innocent. My sister and I would run to Nanny, to Sophie, sometimes even to Father for protection against her irrational moods.

She said nothing more, but stayed by my side. Walking faster, hoping to lose her, I finally looked to my right and mumbled breathlessly to the air, with a hint of irritation, "Why are you here?"

"I am here to ask for your forgiveness," she state forthrightly.

I stopped. Tears added to my confusion. All those years. Forgiveness? That didn't sound like her. After a long pause I was able to answer.

"Forgiveness? Yes, yes, I will, but—," I answered quickly, not knowing what I meant, and with a faltering voice amid memories of returning anxieties. "But, who are you? Really? How do I know this is you? Am I making this up?" I asked for a sign. Struggling, I needed something to assure me. This "visitation" was not my expectation. I am not sentimental. I don't need to manifest an imaginary relationship. Or so I thought.

"Oh, Silly," she said endearingly, calling me by my seldom-used nickname. "I've been giving you a sign for years, but you don't see it. I have shown you the number 1111. You are aware of the number, I know you are. That is me, contacting you. You were born at 1111 Park Avenue.

"It's just me, Silly. No need to be frightened." I heard her accent and remembered the time when she had taken me and my broken doll to the doll hospital.

I began to see the shape of my mother, but a different mother from the one I'd known. Such a long time had passed. My childhood world hadn't been safe. Now she seemed kind, soft, round, without the angular lines of her face, the wrinkled, worried brow suggesting irritation. I didn't reach out to her airy presence. I knew I couldn't grab hold of her, and anyway, she had never been much of a hugger.

Stunned, I stopped walking and returned to my sparse guest room at the convent. I wrote down what happened. I turned off the light and looked at the clock.

It said 11:11.

21

The Dance

I wanted to follow Aunt Billie's dance, not Mother's. I wanted my path to look like a collage of rearranged pieces of my character. My Yankee-planted feet would stand alongside the allure of Southern mystery; the comfort of familial rewards would give me safety; and somewhere close would hover the determined and curious spirit of Cactus Pete.

I better understood my meaning of collage one late afternoon while I was with Margeaux in the beauty of Zago, her paper store in downtown Santa Fe. As we sat at the long, narrow table in the spare space, she asked why I was attracted to collage. My method was to print the photographs on transparent Japanese paper, then tear the prints up into pieces that appealed to me.

"When I arrange the pieces, I see the layers of a story and how they belong to each other."

I hesitated in my explanation, slightly unsure of my exact meaning and insecure about describing it to an artist I greatly admired. But the vibrant, trusting connection to Margeaux was easy. Lovely, tall, and slender, with a graceful natural grey streak running through her long hair, she had a quiet, thoughtful presence, and a powerful gleam in her eye. I spoke of my intentions as a photographer, especially in the recent work with the SEWA women in India, how I watched them dig through the rags at the dump.

"What do you think?" I asked Margeaux. "What about defiance in women? Do you think we'll ever confront the patriarchy? Or will we just keep selling out to safety?" Her spirited answers supported my questions, and her own artwork reflected a dedicated passion and soul. Margeaux seemed so true.

Joan and Margeaux

The Magnolia Code

With her aesthetic eye and thoughtful concern, she helped me pick out the Japanese papers that best related to my images. She took my work seriously. I trusted her enough to share a memory. It was Christmas when, at age seven, I asked for a camera. I unwrapped my present, excitedly lined everyone up for the photograph, pushed the button and—to my horror—a yellow plastic duck popped out. I was old enough to know I was supposed to laugh with the others at the fake camera. My little-girl self-worth was crushed. But I didn't cry.

Margeaux and I saw each other every few days, often sitting at her table, covered with art—mine or that of others looking for advice on the combination of papers and their art creations. In many ways she and I were opposites—in presence, in demeanor, in our histories. We discovered with amusement that we had one thing in common. We were both brought up on islands: she on the small, idyllic Treasure Island of Southern California and I on Manhattan.

Surprisingly yet quickly we began to reveal our vulnerable sides, sharing the dark moments we had kept to ourselves. With our façades dissolving into a beguiling trust of attraction, Margeaux asked one day as our hands entwined for the first time, "Shouldn't we just be friends?"

"Why?" I asked, trusting my instinct that this would be a deep relationship. I wanted to find out.

Our future began to unfold. With a merging of our bodies and spirits into a broader, loving world, I heard Terence's throw-away phrase, said to me so long ago in defensive anger, "Some day someone's going to tame you." My relationship with Margeaux was certainly not about taming each other's hopes and desires, or oppressing and dismissing our daring souls; it was about the possibility of facing life's questions. I felt that all those rules—the Magnolia Code—would still be there, but they would now sit in a diminished place, out of sight, over my shoulder.

I remember a Black Madonna moment, how unselfconsciously the Roma women danced, the sleeves of white blousy shirts falling down dancing arms, how long black hair spun around faces in joyous, frenzied turns. In my attraction with Margeaux, I felt the heartbeat of that exotic dance.

Gypsy women dancing

On my birthday we went to Cuba. Arriving in Havana at midnight, we left our luggage in the hotel and quickly went out onto the streets, moving toward the rich strains of the salsa music. It seemed no one slept; the mojito bars were open and music from the dance hall down the street beckoned. Despite my awareness of the poverty, government repression and abuses on the island nation, this midnight moment in the warmth of the sensuous music was about sharing joy with people who rhythmically whirled and twirled. We danced.

It can seem like a sudden lifting of the veil when one person truly sees another. But it's not sudden—the veil is always thin. From my understanding of the Black Madonna, I had begun to allow myself to look within and hear the icon's message, to dare to go into the darkness. My ability to truly see Margeaux came from being able to part my own veils, cross my own boundaries and befriend my own essence. I was accepting paradox and the balance of opposites.

I was reminded of the image I caught in India of two men sitting a few stories up, absurdly positioned on the edges of opposite roofs, intensely rapt in conversation. Perhaps Margeaux and I were like them—comfortably if precariously poised for engagement.

My close friend Joe had told me years ago that I would never belong.

"You're a Bohemian, just like my mother." His words shocked me at first, but they were also flattering—to be compared to his fascinating mother, who was so self-possessed, so independent; I admired her.

"What do you mean I won't belong?" I asked with a mixture of hurt and a subtle taste of future freedom.

"You don't fit in, not into any mold, anyway," Joe answered lightly and with compassion. As we sat in my living room on 77th Street, sipping scotch and water and musing about his comment, he added, "I'm remembering a story you told me of your birthday celebration at Schrafft's when you were about eleven. I think both your mother and your Aunt Billie were there. I remember that because I know they didn't like each other."

"Yes, we were at Schrafft's," I answered, wandering into the memory. I ordered my favorite coffee ice cream sundae. Mother had her usual cherry pie. Billie had a drink. She had to, had to show the façade of pleasantry to Mother, I guess. And she smoked a lot, I remember.

Billie reminded me how much she loved to dance as she slid her present onto my lap. I excitedly opened the black-and-white Saks Fifth Avenue box. Inside was a pair of black patent leather dancing shoes with a Mary Jane strap across the top.

"Oh, they're beautiful! I always wanted patent leather shoes. I love to dance, just like you, Aunt Billie. May I try them on right now?" I exclaimed, already starting to replace my brown Oxfords with the shiny new shoes. "They fit. Look, look, they fit!'"

Why, Billie, that's so sweet of you," Mother said. "And I'm just tickled she got a beautiful little-girl present. You know what John gave her on her last birthday—rhinestone holsters for her Cactus guns! Can you imagine?"

Balanced and engaged

The Magnolia Code

I glanced over at Billie. She gave me a big smile and told Mother that of course she'd seen me twirl those guns into my fancy holsters.

"That's when I knew Cactus was a star," she said.

I wanted them both—the dancing shoes and the holsters—no question. And, for a long moment, the desire for both seemed just right.

Occasionally I look at Billie's quote, written on a little piece of paper I keep in my wallet: "Might as well be yourself, everyone else is taken."

I can hear her say, "Oh, Joanie, our souls will always have longings and wishes, sometimes opposite wishes, but you just embrace them, dance them into a balance, a harmony."

I can see Billie that day in our den as she got up from the chair and began to twirl, her wide black skirt with the red cats on it gently caressing everything in her path.

"See, just like this. Watch me now."

Acknowledgments—With Thanks and Great Appreciation

My sister Alice, my support since forever

Kay Fowler and Nancy Stem of Fresco Books, the tireless, always creative, always thoughtful—with humor—publishers

Extraordinarily patient and sensitive editor, Hollis Walker

My teachers: Melissa Petro of Gotham Writers Workshop, Lauren Whitehurst, Phyllis Theroux, Jennifer Selig and my colleagues from Writing Down the Soul at Pacifica University, my writing friends at The Santa Fe Write Group, Joan Tewkesbury, Candace Walsh, and Tanya Rubinstein

The First Readers: Margeaux Klein, Steve Jimenez, Dick Moe, Leana Melat, Jim Fitzpatrick, Elisabeth Reed, Don Lamm, Tom Wallace, and The Marshall—Peter Decker

Along with: Susan Herter, Mae Martinez, Kristine Rael, Susan and Trenholm Walker, Paul Chitwood, Jane Lahr, Joe Wemple, Louisa Sarofim, Lee Link, Ann Yeomans, Ali MacGraw, Roxana Robinson, Barbara Baker Mallory, Sallie Bingham, Laura Yorke, Joanna Hess, Shermane Billingsley, Bill Chaput, Sandy Fitzpatrick, Leitner Daleen, Julia Moe, Judy Auchincloss, Brian Rosborough, Liz Glassman, Anne Gallagher, Bonnie Joseph, Sheila Vaughn, Alexandra Eldridge, Jean Vanderbilt, Cynthia Nemo, Kay Buxton, Meredith George, Zahra Farman-Farmaian, Claudia Freund, Louise Whitney, Phillip Retzky, David Hawkanson, Victoria Shorr, Steve Reed, Sharon Fernandes, Joanna Hurley, David Law and Bonnie Carleton, Robin Webster, Carol Mancusi Ungaro-Steen, Katie Kitchen and Paul Kovach, Bonnie Joseph, Kathryn and Roger Toll, Singer Rankin, Margaret Mooney, Susie and Wray Herbert